P9-EKR-340

The Love of
French Cooking

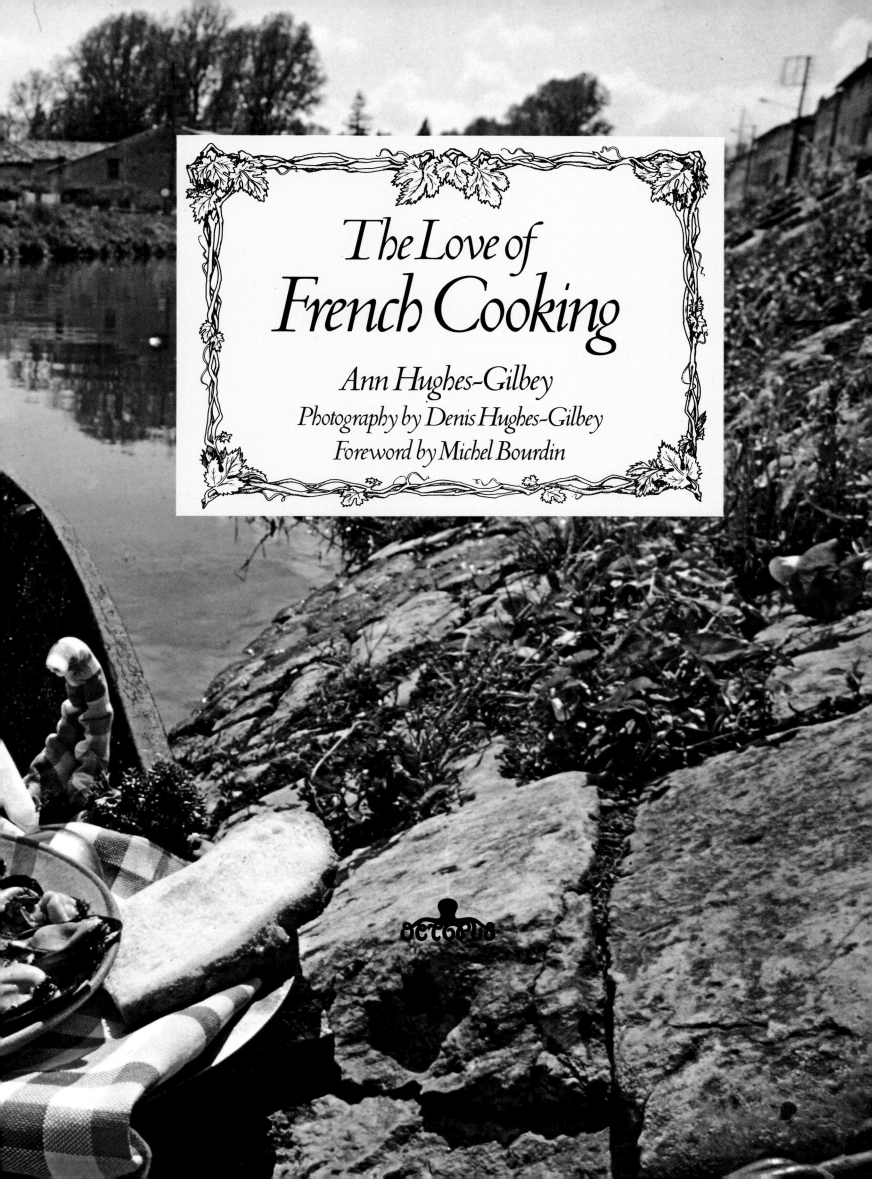

The Love of French Cooking

Ann Hughes-Gilbey

Photography by Denis Hughes-Gilbey

Foreword by Michel Bourdin

FOREWORD

by Michel Bourdin
Chef de Cuisine, The Connaught Hotel

Michel Bourdin is undoubtably one of the finest chefs in the world today. He was second-in-command at the renowned Maxim's restaurant in Paris for several years before bringing his culinary expertise to The Connaught. He is a membre de l'académie de France and a Maître Cuisinier.

Cooking is a question of love. Preparing dishes for others is a truly rewarding pastime; the difficulties we may encounter in the kitchen are soon forgotten when we succeed and are congratulated on our cooking. After all, what can be more satisfying than beautifully cooked food?

Over the centuries the cuisine of France has acquired world-wide supremacy. This reputation *par excellence* can be traced to the French attitude towards food. The French have a tremendous respect for their homeland and the produce it yields. They take pride in transforming this produce into gastronomic delights.

Chefs throughout the provinces of France are continually using their skill, imagination and enthusiasm to create new dishes. Great chefs transcend to the top restaurants and hotels in Paris, London, New York and elsewhere, enabling people outside France to appreciate French gastronomy.

This book on French cooking takes us to the heart of the great Cuisine – to the restaurants and hotels where classic French dishes are created. The well-informed author has wisely selected those simple and elaborate recipes which show that French cooking can be exquisite without being ruinously expensive.

Produce of quality together with the nuance of sauces and seasoning, form the basis of French cooking. Only the freshest fruit and vegetables, the best meat and finest dairy produce should be employed. If a dish is superbly cooked it will taste less than perfect if inferior ingredients are used in the preparation. Sauces must be subtle to enhance but not disguise the flavour of the food to which they are added. It should always be possible to taste every component within a dish.

This original collection of recipes will provide you with a wide range of the dishes prepared all over France. It will inspire you with confidence in your own skills.

Michel Bourdin

First published 1978 by
Octopus Books Limited
59 Grosvenor Street
London W1

© 1978 Octopus Books Limited

ISBN 7064 0695 8

Produced by Mandarin Publishers Limited
22a Westlands Road
Quarry Bay, Hong Kong

Printed in Hong Kong

CONTENTS

Introduction

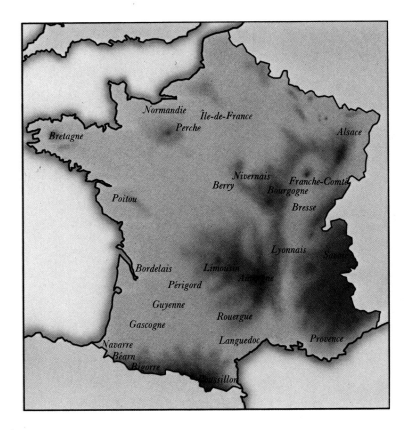

This book was conceived after years of pleasurable motor touring in France. We made no plans, plotted no routes, gave no thought to itineraries; we blew where the wind listed, moving on or staying put as the mood took us. And always we enjoyed the food. We tried the local cheese, the local wines and above all the local dishes – choosing them in preference to the ubiquitous classics, however tempting these might be.

Don't get me wrong: it is not French food we are eulogizing, good though it is. It is the French attitude to food and cooking which gives their cuisine the edge on ours. Take some examples. French apples may be no better than others but they are proud of them. Every French housewife can identify many different kinds by sight and name and she knows which are best for different uses – for eating, for purée, for baking, as accompaniments to meat or to game. The same applies to potatoes and, even more so, to lettuces: there are at least half-a-dozen varieties in the market at any given time and each is picked for its suitability to complement the other ingredients in the planned salad. There are few parts of any food animal with which the French housewife is not familiar and regularly cooks. She also makes use of a huge range of dried pulses, elsewhere left largely to vegetarians.

Edible fungi grow almost everywhere in the world but few people trouble to learn which varieties are safe and good to eat. The French are lucky in having a wide range of choice and they make full use of them: *cèpes, girolles, bolets, chanterelles, oronges, rosés des prés, morilles, trompettes de mort* (excellent despite their sinister name!), *pleurottes* and many others. The *champignon de Paris* (button mushroom) is respected for its delicacy of flavour and used mainly for subtle or pale-coloured dishes and, because of its neat shape, for decoration. Each variety grows in its time and place and,

in due season, family parties take an enjoyable day out at weekends to see how much of this bounty they can gather. Similarly with wild plants; in any country district you will see women combing the fields and hedgerows with basket and knife in hand to cut or dig up goodies for the table or pot.

Look around a large market and see how many levels of cookery are catered for – take geese and ducks for instance. Top of the league is *foie gras*, the huge prized livers of specially fattened birds, found especially in Périgord and Alsace. The breasts of these ducks are particularly sought after as *magrets* and are sold separately but any duck and goose breasts may be offered as special cuts. The legs of *gavé* (fattened birds) are favourites for *confits*. These form the prime cuts but no one would dream of discarding the carcasses and these are also on sale, often with the wings and considerable flesh left on – perfect for *pots-au-feu* or super rich soups. Goose necks, boned and stuffed, are a *spécialité* in Périgord and elsewhere. Cheapest of all are beaks and feet, perhaps not very tempting to eat but still capable of imparting an excellent game flavour to stock.

It will be seen from this that the average French housewife is prepared to spend more time and a little more trouble in preparing her family's meals than the rest of us. If she has a job and lacks time, she can use her extra money to splendid effect by visiting the *traiteur* or cooked-food shop, often part of a *charcuterie*. Here she can buy from an amazing choice of ready-to-heat-up dishes: literally scores of differently prepared meats, rabbit, shellfish; scallops sauced and breadcrumbed in their shells; mussels on skewers dressed for the grill; a selection of hams and cooked meats, sausages and terrines, stuffed cabbage and a dozen or so prepared salads.

The basic differences in regional food were, of course, originally governed geographically, by whatever grew best locally in the days when poor roads meant that 'self-sufficiency' was Hobson's choice. Lush level pastures in the north, spreading westward into Charente, east and south through Lorraine and Bourgogne towards the foot of the Alps, make perfect cattle country. Cattle provide beef, veal and cream; cream means butter and this is the main cooking fat in these regions.

In more broken country, such as is found in Auvergne and south-west through Périgord to the Pyrenees, cattle give way to sheep and to pigs and geese; superbly efficient weight-gainers, these last two make succulent eating and provide excellent fat for cooking. Dried beans, which go particularly well with pork and goose, are commonly found in the main-course dishes of these areas.

Although Alsace hasn't the same geographical disadvantages, it is greatly influenced by German culinary habits and here, too, pork products are popular. It also shares with Périgord a tradition of goose-fattening – presumably the French flair for the good life asserting itself. Where the terrain is really too arid, too steep or too stony to support any sort of pasture and only goats can feed adequately, kid replaces other meats; butter all but disappears. Luckily the olive flourishes in this harsh environment, and its fragrant oil gives the cuisine of Provence, for example, much of its character. Herbs, especially basil and rosemary, grow abundantly in the sunny Southern climate; together with olives, and of course garlic, they are certainly evident in the dishes of Provence and Languedoc.

Woods are plentiful in France and these harbour game, both furred and feathered, which is particularly welcomed for the pot wherever the forest, the altitude or a precipitate landscape makes herding impossible. Every region has rivers, lakes and/or sea – from which almost everything that swims is turned to delicious account. Angling is, after all, a favourite French pastime and abundant trout are further augmented by hatcheries, from which you can buy for your own ultra-fresh supper. Cheese, in magnificent prodigality, is made from the milk of whatever animal – cow, sheep or goat – is to hand. Roquefort, the famous French blue cheese, is prepared from ewes' milk whereas Normandie cattle yield the creamy milk which is used to make Camembert, arguably the finest French soft cheese. Always ask to try the local cheeses wherever you eat or shop.

Clearly the frugality which comes so naturally to the French is a good thing when food prices rocket. It is not just a money-saving grace: it also adds enormous variety to the daily diet – and variety is truly the spice of good eating as well as of life. Perhaps we all get the food we deserve, that we are appreciative enough to want and caring enough to cook. Every Frenchman, though he may never approach a cooker in his life, reckons himself a gastronomic expert and is not afraid to voice his criticism if he considers a dish is less than perfect, which is why you should eat in the restaurant patronized by the locals rather than that which caters exclusively for tourists.

Someone, Brillat-Savarin probably, said that good cooking was 'nothing but eggs, cream, butter and genius' and this is perfectly reflected in classic French cuisine. The first three ingredients were basic currency in every household even if they had no meat. Sobering thought: *foie gras* and truffles were once common peasant fare, as neither had to be bought! Today, the ripples of the *nouvelle cuisine* are becoming waves, and these rich ingredients are used with a lighter hand. But the genius remains and comes to brilliant light on the tables of France's great chefs.

The recipes in this book come from a variety of sources but by far the majority were given by chefs and *patrons* throughout provincial France. We have purposely omitted Paris. There, you can eat the dishes of every region but we preferred to photograph them in their homelands, despite this being a much harder job. A Frenchman probably gets regional food at home; when he eats out, he wants something grander, or classic, which is hard luck on outsiders. Luckily, enterprizing restaurants cater for interested visitors as well – though a few of our dishes were specially made for us.

Our chapter divisions are arbitrary, with deliberately fluid boundaries. Partly to show that they should not be thought of in a strict geographical sense and, partly for fun, we have given our regions their pretty historical names. Apart from the unlikelihood of finding a very few of the ingredients in an ordinary family kitchen, none of the recipes are 'difficult'; most are well within the capabilities of an average competent housewife or bachelor, of either sex, and a great many are simple enough for a beginner.

Apart from its cooking, we love France itself – the country, the people, the way of life. In the small space available (this is after all primarily a book for cooks, not travellers!), we can't really begin to persuade you to our way of thinking but hope you'll want to go and taste 'the real thing' in France as well as making it for yourself.

ANN HUGHES-GILBEY

Normandie, Bretagne, Poitou

English connections of one sort or another are very strong throughout this group of provinces. Normandie was taken over by Norsemen, hence the name, and later produced William the Conqueror who made 1066 the best-known date in English history. More recently, the Normandie beaches meant much to men of many nations; the grief and terror of 1944 have been transformed by time to grave respect and the endless sands are given over now to holiday pleasure.

'Bespectacled' cows browsing in orchards typify Normandie's specialities: butter, cream, more than twenty cheeses, apples, cider and Calvados – that intriguing brandy with a delicious apple bouquet. Add placidly fertile farmland flanked by seas apparently brimming with fish, and you'll see why Normandie has such a reputation for good food. It is also renowned for palaces, abbeys and historic manor houses of a fairytale beauty. Lovely half-timbering adds attraction to buildings, from stately homes to tiny cowsheds, and fascinating chequerboard patterns are made with stone, flint and brick.

When the Romans pulled back to defend Italy against the barbarians, many Celts fled from Britain across the Channel to Bretagne, or 'little Britain', bringing with them place-names such as Penmarch, Locronan and Trezien. Tidal river inlets are *abers* as in Wales, Tristan, Isolde and Merlin live on in local legend; Welsh and Cornish speakers may even understand the patois.

Warm moist weather from the Gulf Stream encourages fruit and vegetables: Breton strawberries, tomatoes, onions, cauliflowers, above all artichokes, are famous throughout Europe. Pancakes, once a peasant staple, proliferate with uncountable fillings to be washed down with *chouchen* (honey wine). The only 'real' Breton wine is Muscadet with 22 varieties! It is considered by many to be the supreme – if not only – accompaniment for seafood. With such an extensive coastline, doubled by thousands of inlets, it's not surprising that fish is a popular comestible in Bretagne – particularly shellfish, with oysters an especial pride. As well as long strands there are smaller coves sheltered by tumbled black rocks below gorse-topped cliffs. Low-built granite villages withstand time and weather, with the graceful pierced church spires lending lightness and beauty.

Poitou and its surroundings belonged to England for many years. Agricultural produce and fish from coastal waters are plentiful in this area with mussels and the delicate *claires* (Marennes oysters) leading the seafood stakes. Towards Bordeaux are enormous vineyards; their wine is unremarkable but it goes to make the king of brandies, Cognac. When visiting Poitou do try *Pineau des Charentes*, a fortified wine apéritif flavoured with Cognac. Here the architectural glory is Romanesque churches built when pilgrimages were regular happenings. You can even see poignant pilgrim graffiti, visible among later scratchings, on the remains of the Hospice at Pons. A flattish area, the scenery is pleasant but unremarkable – save for the *Marais Poitevin* with its miles of tiny canals tunnelling through vaulted trees among floating pastures.

TERRINE DE CANETON AUX NOISETTES

Duck Pâté with Hazelnuts

Metric/Imperial
1 duckling (see recipe)
3 × 15 ml spoons/3 tablespoons Cognac
1 small onion, finely chopped
2 shallots, finely chopped
2 carrots, chopped
sprig of fresh thyme
2–3 bay leaves
6 × 15 ml spoons/6 tablespoons dry white wine
250 g/9 oz lean veal
0.5 kg/1 lb 2 oz lean pork
125 g/4½ oz pig's liver
125 g/4½ oz duck livers
2 eggs
75 g/3 oz shelled hazelnuts
salt
freshly ground black pepper
flour for binding (as necessary)
4–5 rashers streaky bacon
50 g/2 oz can foie gras pâté
lard for sealing
TO SERVE:
aspic jelly

American
1 duckling (see recipe)
3 tablespoons Cognac
1 small onion, finely chopped
2 shallots, finely chopped
2 carrots, chopped
sprig of fresh thyme
2–3 bay leaves
6 tablespoons dry white wine
9 oz lean veal
1 lb 2 oz lean pork
4½ oz pig's liver

4½ oz duck livers
2 eggs
½ cup shelled filberts
salt
freshly ground black pepper
flour for binding (as necessary)
4–5 slices bacon
2 oz can foie gras pâté
lard for sealing
TO SERVE:
aspic jelly

Cut the duck open along the back and remove the breasts, taking care to keep them whole. Remove the flesh from the rest of the duck. Set aside 250 g/9 oz of this; the remainder with the carcass can be used for soup or *pot-au-feu.*

Place the duck breasts in a small bowl and cover with the Cognac. Place the reserved duck flesh, onion, shallots, carrots and herbs in another bowl and pour over the wine. Leave both to marinate overnight.

Remove the duck flesh from the wine and mince (grind) together with the veal, pork and livers. Mix well with the onion and shallots from the marinade, the eggs, nuts, salt and pepper. If the mixture seems too wet, stir in a very little flour.

Lay the bacon in the bottom of a terrine and arrange the bay leaves from the marinade on top. Press half of the mixture into the terrine. Coat the duck breasts evenly with the foie gras pâté and place along the centre of the terrine. Press the remaining mixture on top. Cook in a pre-heated moderate oven (180°C/350°F/Gas Mark 4) for 1½ to 2 hours. Allow to cool.

When cold, smooth a layer of lard over the top to seal. To serve turn out onto a plate and surround with chopped aspic jelly.
SERVES 12 TO 15

ÉCLAIRS AU JAMBON

Savoury Éclairs with Ham

The Marine Hotel crouches between the soaring magnificence of the Pont de Tancarville and a crumbling chalk cliff crowned with a 12th Century castle. The busy river traffic on the Seine slides past the windows – a superb accompaniment to a meal.

Metric/Imperial
PÂTE À CHOUX:
100 g/4 oz butter, cut into pieces
pinch of salt
pinch of grated nutmeg
small pinch of sugar
250 ml/8 fl oz water
125 g/4½ oz plain flour, sifted
4 eggs, beaten
FILLING:
50 g/2 oz butter
75 g/3 oz flour
500 ml/18 fl oz milk
100 g/4 oz Gruyère or Cheddar cheese, finely grated
50 g/2 oz mushrooms, chopped and sautéed in a little butter
100 g/4 oz cooked ham, chopped
little chopped truffle (optional)
salt, pepper, nutmeg
TO FINISH:
12 thin slices cooked ham
100 g/4 oz Gruyère or Cheddar cheese, grated
12 thin slices smoked streaky bacon
strips of tomato to garnish

American
PÂTE À CHOUX:
½ cup butter, cut into pieces
pinch of salt
pinch of grated nutmeg
small pinch of sugar
1 cup water
1 cup + 2 tablespoons all-purpose flour
4 eggs, beaten
FILLING:
¼ cup butter
¾ cup flour
2¼ cups milk
1 cup finely grated Gruyère or Cheddar cheese
½ cup chopped mushrooms, sautéed in a little butter
½ cup chopped processed ham
little chopped truffle (optional)
salt, pepper, nutmeg
TO FINISH:
12 thin slices processed ham
1 cup grated Gruyère or Cheddar cheese
12 thin slices bacon
strips of tomato to garnish

Bisque d'Étrilles

To make the *pâte à choux*; place the butter, salt, nutmeg, sugar and water in a saucepan over low heat. When the butter has melted, bring to the boil and add all the flour at once. Beat vigorously until the mixture forms a ball which leaves the sides of the pan clean. Cool slightly, then beat in the eggs, one at a time, until thoroughly mixed.

Place the mixture in a piping bag, fitted with a 2 cm/¾ inch plain nozzle. Pipe 12 lines of dough, about 10 cm/4 inches long, onto greased baking sheets, spacing them well apart. Cook in a preheated hot oven (220°C/425°F/Gas Mark 7) for about 30 minutes or until éclairs are well-puffed, browned and firm to the touch. Make a slit along the side of each one to release the steam and return to the oven for 5 minutes or until crisp. Cut in half, cool on a wire rack and remove any remaining soft dough from the centres of the éclairs.

To make the filling: melt the butter in a saucepan over low heat. Beat in the flour and cook for 1 to 2 minutes. Stir in the milk gradually, then bring to the boil, stirring constantly, and cook until the sauce is thick and smooth. Add the cheese, mushrooms, ham and truffle, if used. Season to taste with salt, pepper and nutmeg. Allow to cool.

When cold, fill the éclairs with two-thirds of the sauce and wrap each one in a slice of ham. Coat with some of the remaining sauce and roll in the grated cheese. Wrap a slice of bacon around the middle of each. Brown in the top of a very hot oven (240°C/475°F/Gas Mark 9) immediately before serving. Garnish with strips of tomato and serve with watercress. Allow one éclair per person for an entrée or two for a main course.

MAKES 12 ÉCLAIRS

BISQUE D'ÉTRILLES

Crab Soup

My school dictionary gave *étrille* as meaning 'curry comb' – but to French housewives it means those little red crabs which the French cook and we don't . . .

Metric/Imperial
2 kg/4½–4¾ lb small crabs, crayfish or
    other crustaceans
450 ml/¾ pint Muscadet or other dry
    white wine
4 × 15 ml spoons/4 tablespoons Cognac
1.5 × 15 ml spoons/1½ tablespoons oil
25 g/1 oz butter
2 onions, roughly chopped
6 cloves garlic, crushed
bouquet garni
sprig of fresh tarragon (optional)
250 g/9 oz tomato purée
salt
freshly ground black pepper

Éclairs au Jambon

5 × 15 ml spoons/5 tablespoons double
cream
TO SERVE:
few slices stale bread, cubed
2 cloves garlic, finely chopped
oil for shallow frying

American
4½–4¾ lb small crabs, écrivisses or other
    crustaceans
2 cups Muscadet or other dry white wine
4 tablespoons Cognac
1½ tablespoons oil
2 tablespoons butter
2 onions, roughly chopped
6 cloves garlic, crushed
bouquet garni
sprig of fresh tarragon (optional)
¾ cup tomato paste

salt
freshly ground black pepper
5 tablespoons heavy cream
TO SERVE:
few slices stale bread, cubed
2 cloves garlic, finely chopped
oil for shallow frying

Crush the crabs with a rolling pin and place them in a large pan. Add all the remaining soup ingredients, except the cream. Bring to the boil and simmer covered, stirring frequently, for 1 hour. Strain the soup.

Mix the bread with the garlic and sauté in the oil until golden brown and crisp. Drain on kitchen paper. Just before serving, stir the cream into the hot soup. Serve the garlic-flavoured croûtons separately.

SERVES 6 TO 8

MOUCLADE MARAÎCHINE

Creamed Mussels

The Marais Poitevin is one of the most beautiful and intriguing of France's 'unknown' treasures. The agricultural market town of Niort was once a port but the centuries have silted up the bay on which it stood, leaving nearly 200,000 acres of fertile flatland and marsh, drained by a myriad of little canals. Along the larger of these, cattle and horses are taken in small flat boats to graze through the summer on fields which are really floating islands.

Coulon is one of the tiny towns from which you can begin a trip along these waterways and you can eat before or afterwards at Restaurant au Marais.

Metric/Imperial
0.5 kg/1 lb mussels, scrubbed and washed thoroughly
1–2 onions, chopped
large handful of chopped fresh parsley
1–2 × 5 ml spoons/1–2 teaspoons curry powder
¼ teaspoon sea salt
250 ml/8 fl oz dry white wine
250 ml/8 fl oz double cream
chopped fresh parsley to garnish

American
1 lb mussels, scrubbed and washed thoroughly
1–2 onions, chopped
large handful of chopped fresh parsley
1–2 teaspoons curry powder
¼ teaspoon sea salt
1 cup dry white wine
1 cup heavy cream
chopped fresh parsley to garnish

Put all the ingredients in a large saucepan and cook over a brisk heat, turning frequently, until all the mussels are open: 5 to 6 minutes.

Take the mussels out of the pan with a perforated spoon. Leave the sauce on a low heat to reduce to a thick creamy consistency. Discard the empty half-shells and arrange the mussels in their half-shells on a serving dish.

Pour the hot sauce over and sprinkle with chopped parsley. Serve immediately with toast, as an entrée.

SERVES 2

BROCHETTE DE COQUILLES ST JACQUES

Scallop 'Kebabs'

In 1694 the British and Dutch tried unsuccessfully to land an invasion force at Camaret-sur-Mer, on the tip of the Crozon Peninsular. In Napoleonic times, the American Robert Fulton tried to make a go of his submarine here! Modern visitors follow more peaceful pursuits: sailing, skin-diving and sampling the local shellfish. The Brest Roadstead, just to the north, is particularly famous for scallops; grilled on skewers these make a popular luncheon dish.

Metric/Imperial
20 scallops, shelled and halved if large
8 small tomatoes, halved
225 g/8 oz belly pork or smoked streaky bacon, cubed
oil for basting

Brochette de Coquilles St Jacques

American
20 scallops, shelled and halved if large
8 small tomatoes, halved
½ lb salt pork or bacon, cubed
oil for basting

Thread the scallops, tomatoes and meat alternately onto 4 kebab skewers. Brush with oil and cook under a medium grill (broiler) for about 4 to 5 minutes on each side, basting frequently.

Serve on a bed of lettuce, with plain boiled rice and lemon slices.
SERVES 4

SAUCE À L'AMÉRICAINE

This is not at all difficult – but only practical when you are serving shellfish such as lobsters, crabs, crayfish (écrevisses), shrimps etc.

Metric/Imperial
two handfuls of crushed shellfish legs, claws, shells etc.
4 × 15 ml spoons/4 tablespoons oil
3 onions, chopped
2 shallots, chopped
3 cloves garlic, chopped
1 wine glass of Cognac
1 bottle dry white wine
bouquet garni
6 tomatoes, skinned, seeded and roughly chopped
4 × 15 ml spoons/4 tablespoons tomato purée
salt
freshly ground black pepper
pinch of cayenne pepper

American
two handfuls of crushed shellfish legs, claws, shells etc.
4 tablespoons oil
3 onions, chopped
2 shallots, chopped
3 cloves garlic, chopped
1 wine glass of Cognac
1 bottle dry white wine
bouquet garni
6 tomatoes, skinned, seeded and roughly chopped
4 tablespoons tomato paste
salt
freshly ground black pepper
pinch of cayenne pepper

Fry the shells, etc., in the oil over a brisk heat, turning frequently, for 5 to 10 minutes, until browned. Lower the heat, add the onions, shallots and garlic and cook until they become transparent. Add the remaining ingredients, bring to the boil, then simmer for 30 minutes.

Strain and serve with shellfish.
MAKES ABOUT 450 ML/¾ PINT/2 CUPS

Pétoncles Farcies Grillées

PÉTONCLES FARCIES GRILLÉES

Grilled Stuffed Shellfish

Pétoncles are shellfish like miniature scallops, complete with shells and tiny corals. I've never seen them anywhere else, but this recipe is exactly right for cockles or any similar small shellfish. As with all shellfish, they must be absolutely fresh.

Metric/Imperial
60 chosen shellfish (depending on size)
STUFFING:
100 g/4 oz butter, softened
3–4 cloves garlic, very finely chopped
large handful of chopped fresh parsley
salt
freshly ground black pepper
juice of ½ lemon
25 g/1 oz fresh breadcrumbs

American
60 chosen shellfish (depending on size)
STUFFING:
½ cup butter, softened
3–4 cloves garlic, very finely chopped
large handful of chopped fresh parsley
salt
freshly ground black pepper
juice of ½ lemon
½ cup fresh bread crumbs

Clean the shellfish thoroughly in several changes of cold water. Open them with a sharp knife and discard the empty half-shells.

Beat the butter with the garlic, parsley, salt, pepper and lemon juice. Place a small spoonful on each shell. Lay the shellfish on a baking sheet or on individual flame-proof plates. Lightly sprinkle with bread-crumbs and cook under a preheated grill (broiler) for about 5 minutes. Serve immediately, accompanied by French bread and butter.
SERVES 4 TO 6

HOMARD BRETON GRILLÉ À LA CORNOUAILLAISE

Grilled Lobster in Rich Sauce

Adolphe Bosser has a special place in our hearts as he was the very first chef-patron we ever approached to cook something for us to photograph. He is steadily upgrading his delightful quayside Hotel de Guyen at Audierne. Breton music is one of his interests and he stages occasional musical evenings during the season, when you can enjoy performances by local *baguades* (a group of bagpipe, bombard and cornet). This is the speciality he made for us.

Metric/Imperial

250 g/9 oz tomatoes, seeded and roughly chopped
2 × 15 ml spoons/2 tablespoons finely chopped shallots
250 ml/8 fl oz dry white wine
salt
1 live lobster, weighing about 0.75 kg/1¾ lb
freshly ground black pepper
75 g/3 oz butter
50 g/2 oz flour
450 ml/¾ pint double cream
150 ml/¼ pint brandy
2 × 5 ml spoons/2 teaspoons Dijon mustard
1 × 15 ml spoon/1 tablespoon chopped fresh tarragon
2 × 5 ml spoons/2 teaspoons finely grated Parmesan cheese

American

1 cup seeded and roughly chopped tomatoes
2 tablespoons finely chopped shallots
1 cup dry white wine
salt
1 live lobster, weighing about 1¾ lb
freshly ground black pepper
⅓ cup butter
½ cup flour
2 cups heavy cream
⅔ cup brandy
2 teaspoons Dijon mustard
1 tablespoon chopped fresh tarragon
2 teaspoons finely grated Parmesan cheese

Place the tomatoes, shallots, wine and a pinch of salt in a pan over moderate heat. Simmer, uncovered, until the mixture has reduced and thickened and the vegetables have softened.

Kill the lobster by giving it a sharp blow on the top of the head. Using a knife with a serrated edge, split it in two lengthwise through the head, body and tail. Discard the grey sac in the head and the thin black line running through the body and tail. Detach the claws and place them together with the halved lobster in a roasting tin. Sprinkle the flesh with salt and pepper and dot with half of the butter. Cook in a preheated moderate oven (180°C/350°F/Gas Mark 4) for about 15 minutes, basting the lobster frequently with the pan juices to ensure the flesh does not become dry.

Blend together the flour and 25 g/1 oz/ 2 tablespoons of the remaining butter to make a *beurre manié*. Bring the cream just to the boil in a pan, beat in the *beurre manié*, a small piece at a time, and cook gently, stirring for 10 minutes. When the tomato mixture is reduced to a thick pulp, stir in the cream then strain through a sieve, pressing as much pulp through as possible. The sauce should be a rich, creamy consistency.

Grind a little more black pepper onto the lobster pieces, pour on all but 1 × 15 ml spoon/1 tablespoon of the brandy and set alight, basting until the flames are extinguished. Work the mustard into the sauce, stir in the tarragon and pour over the lobster. Cook over a moderate heat for 2 to 3 minutes, spooning the sauce over the lobster all the time.

Pick out the lobster pieces and arrange on a warmed flameproof serving dish; keep hot while reducing the sauce. When thick and smooth, refine the sauce by beating in the remaining butter in small flakes; this gives it a final gloss. Spoon over lobster; sprinkle lightly with Parmesan cheese and flash under a very hot grill (broiler) until browned and sizzling. Sprinkle with a few drops of brandy before serving.

An impressive dish to serve at a dinner party. It is quite rich and should be followed by a light dessert.

SERVES 2

Homard Breton Grillé à la Cornouaillaise

LAPIN AU CIDRE
Rabbit in Cider

Metric/Imperial
3 rabbit joints – hindquarters and saddle
50 g/2 oz butter
225 g/8 oz shallots, very finely chopped
sprig of fresh thyme
salt
freshly ground black pepper
5 × 15 ml spoons/5 tablespoons
*   Calvados, warmed*
450 ml/¾ pint dry cider
2–3 tart dessert apples (Belle de Boskope
*   or Granny Smith)*
40 g/1½ oz butter

American
3 rabbit joints – hindquarters and saddle
¼ cup butter
2 cups very finely chopped shallots
sprig of fresh thyme
salt
freshly ground black pepper
5 tablespoons Calvados, warmed
2 cups hard dry cider
2–3 dessert apples
3 tablespoons butter

Wipe the rabbit joints. Melt the butter in a flameproof casserole or heavy-based pan and fry the rabbit until evenly browned. Add the shallots and thyme, and cook gently, covered, until the shallots are soft but not coloured. Season with salt and pepper. Pour in the warmed Calvados and set alight.

When the flames have died down, pour in the cider and simmer, uncovered, until the meat is very tender; about 45 minutes, depending on the age and size of the rabbit joints. Meanwhile, peel, core and quarter the apples and sauté gently in the butter until just soft.

Put the joints and apple quarters on a warmed serving dish, strain the cooking liquor over the rabbit.
SERVES 3

SALADE CAUCHOISE
Normandy Salad

Metric/Imperial
1 curly lettuce
2 large slices cooked ham, roughly
*   chopped*
12 walnut halves
1 large or 2 small dessert apples, cored
*   and sliced*
DRESSING:
1 × 5 ml spoon/1 teaspoon French
*   mustard*

1 × 2.5 ml spoon/¼ teaspoon salt
freshly ground black pepper
1 × 15 ml spoon/1 tablespoon cider
*   vinegar*
3 × 15 ml spoons/3 tablespoons single
*   cream*

American
1 curly lettuce
2 large slices processed ham, roughly
*   chopped*
12 walnut halves
1 large or 2 small dessert apples, cored
*   and sliced*

DRESSING:
1 teaspoon French mustard
¼ teaspoon salt
freshly ground black pepper
1 tablespoon cider vinegar
3 tablespoons light cream

Mix the lettuce leaves, ham, walnuts and apples in a serving bowl. Prepare the dressing by shaking the ingredients together in a screw-top jar. Pour over the salad and toss the ingredients just before serving.
SERVES 4

Lapin au Cidre, Salade Cauchoise

CÔTES D'AGNEAU À L'ESTRAGON

Lamb Chops with Tarragon

M. Pommier served this dish for us beautifully trimmed, with the lamb chops arranged criss-cross fashion.

Metric/Imperial

4 lamb cutlets
25 g/1 oz butter
2 × 15 ml spoons/2 tablespoons oil
handful of tarragon leaves, chopped
2 × 15 ml spoons/2 tablespoons dry white wine
3 × 15 ml spoons/3 tablespoons fond blanc (see page 94)
1 × 15 ml spoon/1 tablespoon cream
salt
freshly ground black pepper
GARNISH:
2–3 lettuces, roughly chopped
50 g/2 oz butter, cut into pieces
2 small onions
1 sugar lump
bouquet garni
salt, pepper
1 × 5 ml spoon/1 teaspoon flour

American

4 lamb rib chops
2 tablespoons butter
2 tablespoons oil
handful of tarragon leaves, chopped
2 tablespoons dry white wine
3 tablespoons fond blanc (see page 94)
1 tablespoon cream
salt
freshly ground black pepper
GARNISH:
2–3 lettuces, roughly chopped
¼ cup butter, cut into pieces
2 small onions
1 sugar lump
bouquet garni
salt, pepper
1 teaspoon flour

Prepare the garnish first: layer the chopped lettuce and three-quarters of the butter in a heavy-based pan. Make a hollow in the centre and put in the onions, sugar and bouquet garni. Sprinkle with salt and pepper. Cover and cook very gently for 30–45 minutes.

Meanwhile trim off any excess fat from the chops. Heat the butter and oil in a frying pan (skillet) and fry the lamb chops with the tarragon, turning them once. The meat is ready when brown on the outside but pink in the centre. Transfer to a serving dish and keep warm. Pour off most of the cooking juices from the pan. Add the wine to the pan and boil until reduced by half. Stir in the *fond blanc* and, when thoroughly mixed, the cream. Strain the sauce, and set aside the tarragon.

Taste and season with salt and pepper.

To complete the garnish; remove the onions and bouquet garni from the lettuce. Work the flour with the remaining butter and add this *beurre manié* a little at a time to the lettuce, stirring, then bring back to the boil.

Arrange the lamb and lettuce on a heated serving dish, surround with a little of the sauce and serve the rest separately. Spread a little of the reserved tarragon over each lamb chop and serve the dish immediately.

SERVES 2

AIGUILLETTE DE CANARD AU CIDRE

Duck Breasts in Cider

This dish needs sharp dessert apples to complement the extreme richness of the sauce.

Metric/Imperial

2 duck breasts, thickly sliced
100 g/4 oz butter
6 × 15 ml spoons/6 tablespoons dry cider
3 × 15 ml spoons/3 tablespoons fond blanc (see page 94)
salt
freshly ground black pepper
GARNISH:
2–3 dessert apples, peeled, cored and quartered
butter for shallow frying

American

2 duck breasts, thickly sliced
½ cup butter
6 tablespoons hard dry cider
3 tablespoons fond blanc (see page 94)
salt
freshly ground black pepper
GARNISH:
2–3 dessert apples, peeled, cored and quartered
butter for shallow frying

Sauté the duck slices in half of the butter over fairly high heat, turning occasionally, for a few minutes; the meat should be pink for maximum flavour and tenderness. Transfer the meat to a serving dish and keep warm. Pour off the fat, and *déglacez* with the cider. Boil until reduced almost completely. Stir in the *fond blanc*, taste and season with salt and pepper. Off the heat, add the remaining butter, stirring briskly with a wooden spoon to yield a smooth sauce.

Meanwhile cook the apple quarters in a little butter, turning carefully once or twice, until just tender. Pour the sauce over the duck and serve the apples as an accompaniment.

SERVES 2

JAMBON AU CIDRE

Ham in Cider

The mellow old stone buildings of the Manoir d'Hastings shelter inside the demesne wall of a 17th Century priory. This means alas that, though it is named after the famous 1066 battle, it cannot really claim that William the Conqueror slept there on his way to England!

This typical old Normandy recipe is a speciality at the Manoir. It is often accompanied by a dish of leeks and potatoes, boiled until tender, then diced and tossed in a creamy Béchamel sauce (see page 94).

Metric/Imperial

1 ham, weighing about 3 kg/6½ lb
1–2 bottles cider, depending on size and shape of pan
100 g/4 oz butter
6 × 15 ml spoons/6 tablespoons cider vinegar
salt
white pepper

American

1 ham, weighing about 6½ lb
1–2 bottles of cider, depending on size and shape of pan
½ cup butter
6 tablespoons cider vinegar
salt
white pepper

Soak the ham in several changes of cold water for 24 hours. Put it in a large saucepan, cover with cider and bring slowly to the boil. Skim well, lower the heat and simmer gently until the ham is tender; 2¼ to 2½ hours – allow 20 minutes per 0.5 kg/1 lb. Leave to cool in the cooking liquor.

Lift the ham out of the pan, trim and cut into slices. Heat three-quarters of the butter in a frying pan (skillet) and sauté the ham slices, allowing them to colour very slightly. Transfer to a serving dish and keep warm. *Déglacez* the pan with the cider vinegar, add 250 ml/8 fl oz/1 cup of the ham cooking liquor and reduce over a brisk heat until syrupy. Taste and add salt and pepper as needed. Whisk in the remaining butter, a little at a time, to 'polish' the sauce. Spoon over the ham immediately before serving.

SERVES 12 TO 15

Aiguillette de Canard au Cidre, Côtes d'Agneau à l'Estragon, Crêpes aux Pommes (page 18), Calcoq (page 21)

CRÈME PÂTISSIÈRE

Confectioners' Custard

A delicious *crème* to serve with fruit or as a filling for *crêpes*, choux buns or sponge cakes.

Metric/Imperial
500 ml/18 fl oz milk
1 vanilla pod or a few drops of vanilla essence
125 g/4½ oz sugar
3 egg yolks
25 g/1 oz plain flour
25 g/1 oz cornflour

American
2¼ cups milk
1 vanilla bean or a few drops of vanilla extract
½ cup + 1 tablespoon sugar
3 egg yolks
¼ cup all-purpose flour
¼ cup cornstarch

Put the milk, vanilla pod and half of the sugar in a pan and bring slowly to the boil. Take off the heat and allow the pod to infuse.

Whisk the rest of the sugar with the egg yolks in a basin. Sift in the flour and cornflour and whisk until smooth. Little by little add the hot milk, whisking all the time. (Add vanilla essence at this stage if used.)

Return to the pan and, stirring briskly all the time, bring to the boil and cook very gently for 1 minute. If the *crème* is to be used cold, cover with greaseproof (waxed) paper to prevent a skin forming during cooling.

MAKES ABOUT 600 ML/1 PINT/2½ CUPS

CRÊPES

Pancakes

Sweet pancakes are generally better made as thin as possible so the batter should be of a thin cream consistency. If the pancakes are to be stuffed they should be slightly more robust, with a little less liquid in the batter, but not too thick or the pancakes will tend to break and taste doughy.

Metric/Imperial
100 g/4 oz plain flour
pinch of salt
1 egg
300 ml/½ pint milk
fat or oil for frying

American
1 cup all-purpose flour
pinch of salt
1 egg
1¼ cups milk
fat or oil for frying

Sift the flour and salt into a bowl, make a well in the centre and add the egg. Pour in about one-third of the milk. Gradually draw the flour into the liquid and beat with a wooden spoon or whisk until smooth. Beat in enough of the remaining liquid to thin the batter to the required consistency.

Heat a little fat or oil in a 12–18 cm/5–7 inch heavy-based frying pan (skillet) with sloping sides. When the fat is very hot, but not smoking, pour in a little batter, tilting the pan to allow the batter to spread and cover the base evenly. Cook for 1 to 2 minutes, until the underside is browned. Toss or turn the pancake with a palette knife and cook the other side.

Turn out onto greaseproof (waxed) paper. Repeat until all the batter is used. If the pancakes are to be eaten straight away, sprinkle with lemon juice and sugar or spread with *crème pâtissière* (see left) or chosen filling and roll up. Alternatively stack, interleaved with greaseproof (waxed) paper, until required.

MAKES 8 TO 12

LE CHANTECLER

Layered Coffee Gâteau

Metric/Imperial
MACAROON:
8 egg whites
125 g/4½ oz ground almonds
200 g/7 oz caster sugar
25 g/1 oz plain flour
SPONGE:
3 eggs
75 g/3 oz caster sugar
75 g/3 oz plain flour, sifted
BUTTER CREAM:
225 g/8 oz sugar
4 × 15 ml spoons/4 tablespoons water
2 egg yolks
225 g/8 oz butter, softened
2–3 × 5 ml spoons/2–3 teaspoons coffee essence
small glass of rum for sprinkling

American
MACAROON:
8 egg whites
1 cup + 2 tablespoons ground almonds
¾ cup + 2 tablespoons superfine sugar
¼ cup all-purpose flour
SPONGE:
3 eggs
⅓ cup sugar
¾ cup all-purpose flour, sifted
BUTTER CREAM:
1 cup sugar
4 tablespoons water
2 egg yolks
1 cup softened butter
2–3 teaspoons coffee extract
small glass of rum for sprinkling

To make the macaroon; whisk the egg whites until stiff. Fold in the ground almonds, sugar and flour evenly. Divide the mixture equally between two greased and floured 23 cm/9 inch sandwich tins (cake layer pans). Bake in a preheated cool oven (150°C/300°F/Gas Mark 2) for 30 minutes. Cool on a wire rack.

For the sponge; whisk the eggs and sugar in a bowl over a pan of hot water until the mixture is pale and thick enough to leave a trail. Carefully fold in the flour. Pour into a buttered and floured 23 cm/9 inch shallow cake tin and bake in a preheated moderately hot oven (190°C/375°F/Gas Mark 5) for 15 to 20 minutes or until risen and firm. Turn out and cool on a wire rack.

To make the butter cream; dissolve the sugar in the water over low heat, stirring constantly. Then boil steadily, without stirring until the syrup reaches a temperature of 116°C/240°F (or until a little of the mixture dropped into a cup of cold water, forms a small ball when rolled between the fingers and thumb). Remove from the heat immediately. Beat the egg yolks in a deep bowl and pour in the hot syrup in a thin stream, whisking constantly. Continue to whisk until the mixture is cool and thick. Gradually beat the egg syrup into the butter and add coffee essence to taste.

To assemble; place one macaroon layer on a serving plate and spread with a layer of butter cream. Place the sponge on top, sprinkle with rum then cover with butter cream. Top with the other macaroon layer and spread the remaining butter cream over the top and sides, using a fork to mark a pattern. Chill before serving.

This cake will keep in the refrigerator for up to 3 days.

MAKES ONE 23 CM/9 INCH GÂTEAU

CRÊPES AUX POMMES

Apple Pancakes

Metric/Imperial
CRÊPE BATTER:
1 egg + 3 yolks
50 g/2 oz sugar
150 g/5 oz plain flour, sifted
25 g/1 oz butter, melted
2 × 15 ml spoons/2 tablespoons oil
150 ml/¼ pint milk

unsalted butter for shallow frying
3 apples, peeled, cored and thinly sliced
TO SERVE:
150 ml/¼ pint Calvados, warmed (optional)
double cream, whipped (optional)
caster sugar for dredging

Le Chantecler, Terrine de Caneton aux Noisettes (page 10)

American

CRÊPE BATTER:

1 egg + 3 yolks
¼ cup sugar
1¼ cups all-purpose flour, sifted
2 tablespoons melted butter
2 tablespoons oil
⅔ cup milk

sweet butter for shallow frying
3 apples, peeled, cored and thinly sliced

TO SERVE:

⅔ cup Calvados, warmed (optional)
heavy cream, whipped (optional)
sugar for dredging

Beat the eggs with the sugar until pale and fluffy. Carefully fold in the sifted flour. Beat in the melted butter and oil, and finally the milk; the mixture should be smooth and creamy.

Melt 25 g/1 oz/2 tablespoons unsalted (sweet) butter in a frying pan (skillet) and put in the apple slices. Cook gently, turning carefully from time to time, until soft but not broken up.

Melt a knob of butter in a cast-iron frying pan (skillet). Pour in batter to a depth of 5 mm/¼ inch and cook over a low heat for 30 seconds. Spread the apples over this, then cover with the rest of the batter. Cook in a preheated moderate oven (180°C/350°F/Gas Mark 4) for about 5 minutes, until well risen and firm. Turn the pancake over carefully and return to the oven for a few minutes to brown the other side.

Serve direct from the pan; if preferred, *flambez* with warmed Calvados. Serve with cream, according to taste, and hand sugar separately.

SERVES 4

TARTE NORMANDE

Normandy Apple Tart

Familiarly known as *La Normande*, this is an individual whole apple tart, capped with a small pancake and flavoured with Calvados. Thick Normandy cream adds a last touch of delicious self-indulgence.

Metric/Imperial

PÂTE SUCRÉE:
225 g/8 oz plain flour
pinch of salt
4 egg yolks
110 g/4 oz butter, softened
110 g/4 oz caster sugar

100 g/4 oz sugar
4 × 15 ml spoons/4 tablespoons water
6 dessert apples, peeled and cored
Crème pâtissière (see page 18 –
  ½ quantity)
6 small crêpes (see page 18 –
  ½ quantity)
6 × 15 ml spoons/6 tablespoons
  Calvados, warmed
150 ml/¼ pint cream, to serve

American

PÂTE SUCRÉE:
2 cups all-purpose flour
pinch of salt
4 egg yolks
½ cup softened butter
½ cup sugar

½ cup sugar
4 tablespoons water
6 dessert apples, peeled and cored
Crème pâtissière (see page 18 –
  ½ quantity)
6 small crêpes (see page 18 –
  ½ quantity)
6 tablespoons Calvados, warmed
⅔ cup cream, to serve

To prepare the *pâte sucrée*; sift the flour and salt onto a working surface, or preferably a marble slab. Make a well in the centre and put in the egg yolks, butter and sugar. Using the fingertips of one hand, knead the centre ingredients until thoroughly blended. Gradually work in the flour and knead the pastry lightly with the fingertips until smooth. Leave to rest in the refrigerator for at least 15 minutes.

Kouign-Amann

Place the sugar and water in a saucepan over low heat and stir until the sugar has dissolved. Add the whole apples. Cover and cook very gently until tender; about 30 minutes, turning the apples and spooning the syrup over them from time to time.

Meanwhile roll out the pastry thinly and use to line six 10 cm/4 inch fluted flan tins. Line the pastry cases with foil and dried beans. Bake blind in a preheated moderately hot oven (190°C/375°F/Gas Mark 5) for 10 minutes. Remove beans and foil and bake for a further 5 minutes until the pastry is lightly browned. Allow to cool.

To assemble; spoon 1 or 2 × 15 ml spoons/1 or 2 tablespoons *crème pâtissière* into each pastry case. Place an apple on top and coat with a little of the syrup. Cover with a pancake. Place each flan on a plate and, as you serve, pour a little Calvados over the pancakes and ignite. Each diner can then douse the flames with a spoonful of cream.
SERVES 6

KOUIGN-AMANN

Breton Pâtisserie

Of all the super Breton pâtisserie, this is the one we liked best. Its name seems to have no translation, even into French. To say that it tastes something like a croissant streaked and glazed with toffee is a poor description of something so delicious. Guaranteed to shrink the waistband!

Metric/Imperial
175 g/6 oz plain flour
2.5 ml spoon/½ teaspoon sea salt
15 g/½ oz fresh yeast
150 ml/¼ pint warm water
100 g/4 oz butter, softened (see recipe)
100 g/4 oz sugar
milk to glaze

American
1½ cups all-purpose flour
½ teaspoon sea salt
½ cake compressed yeast
⅔ cup warm water
½ cup butter, softened (see recipe)
½ cup sugar
milk to glaze

Sift 100 g/4 oz/1 cup of the flour and the salt into a heap on the working surface; preferably marble. Blend the yeast with 2 × 15 ml spoons/2 tablespoons of the water. Make a well in the centre of the flour and add the yeast liquid. Add the remaining liquid gradually, drawing the flour into the liquid using the fingertips. This will yield a very sticky dough which must be kneaded with the fingertips until it becomes elastic.

Gradually incorporate the remaining flour to give a smooth, manageable dough. Knead thoroughly, using one hand, for 3 minutes or until the dough is quite smooth and elastic in texture.

Press the dough out to a rectangle, about 2 cm/1 inch thick and spread with the butter, which should ideally be of the same consistency as the dough. Sprinkle the sugar on top. Fold into three. Give the dough a quarter turn and press the edges together to seal. Roll out to a rectangle. Repeat the folding and rolling three times more.

Press the dough into a shallow 18 cm/ 7 inch greased cake tin. Brush with milk and mark a criss-cross pattern over the top with a sharp knife. Leave to rise in a warm place for 20 minutes. Bake in a preheated moderately hot oven (200°C/ 400°F/Gas Mark 6) for 30 minutes or until well-risen and golden brown on top. Turn onto a wire rack.

This Breton pâtisserie is best eaten while still warm.

MAKES ONE 18 CM/7 INCH ROUND
PÂTISSERIE

CALCOQ

Normandy Coffee

Madame Pommier swears she keeps right out of the kitchen but she does make this pleasant after-dinner drink. It is virtually Gaelic Coffee made with Calvados. The freshly made coffee should be very strong, but not bitter.

Metric/Imperial
FOR EACH PERSON:
1 small cup of black coffee
2 × 15 ml spoons/2 tablespoons Calvados
1 × 5 ml spoon/1 teaspoon sugar syrup (see below)
1 × 5 ml spoon/1 teaspoon caster sugar
2 × 15 ml spoons/2 tablespoons double cream

American
FOR EACH PERSON:
1 small cup of black coffee
2 tablespoons Calvados
1 teaspoon sugar syrup (see below)
1 teaspoon sugar
2 tablespoons heavy cream

Pour a coffee cupful of very hot water into each serving glass or cup so as to warm just to the level to which the black coffee will reach. When the coffee is ready, discard the hot water and pour in the black coffee; quickly add the Calvados, syrup and sugar and stir.

Now pour the cream over the back of a spoon on to the top of the coffee and serve immediately.

SERVES 1

For sugar syrup:
Place 4 × 15 ml spoons/4 tablespoons sugar in a small pan with 5 × 15 ml spoons/ 5 tablespoons water. Heat gently to dissolve the sugar, then bring to the boil and boil steadily for 2 to 3 minutes. These quantities will yield enough sugar syrup for 6 to 8 servings of *Calcoq*.

Breton lady selling artichokes from her market stall in Douarnenez

Aquitaine: Bordelais, Périgord, Guyenne, Gascogne

Roman *Aquitania* (land of waters) took in much of south-western France. Centuries later, it was the dowry of Eleanor, that formidable lady who married two kings and bore two more. When she married England's future Henry II, it was added to England's French possessions; then the name meant 'English France', which stretched from the Channel to the Pyrenees. Lovely, dignified Bordeaux was first made famous by that early 'English connection', when our appetite for clairet did so much to establish the area's great vinous reputation. Though finally reclaimed by the French as long ago as 1453, the region is still littered with English *bastides* (beautiful old towns around an arcaded square) and English place-names such as Liborne and Hastingues. Périgord, with its castled hills and exquisite valleys, is again home to hundreds of English 'settlers'.

In the south are the Landes, once a hellish desert of sandy swampland. Whatever the French may have thought of him otherwise, Napoleon III did them inestimable service when he had this nasty place drained, creating the vast mysterious pine forests which cover it today. Their cool depths shelter innumerable holiday homes and semi-salt lakes which make safe boating and bathing places for families. More experienced swimmers have the run of over 100 miles of clean sandy Atlantic beaches.

This is the land of the goose: geese and ducks are fattened for *foie gras* and goose fat is a basic in the region's cookery. Périgord is also renowned for that ultimate in gastronomic treats – the truffle. Ruinously expensive even here, a little truffle luckily goes a long way, and gathering them must surely be the most entertaining husbandry known. From December through February trained dog or pig *chercheuses* quarter the bare oak-woods in quest of these odd-looking blackish nuggets. Winter in Périgord can be magical and our favourite market of the year is in the picturesque old square in Sarlat on the last Saturday before Christmas. It is filled with geese and *foie gras* and other goodies, and redolent with the truffles' unique bouquet.

Arcachon, site of the world's biggest sand dune, is an important centre for oysters and pretty little red mullet. In the Gironde estuary the *spécialité* is lamprey of which King John died of a surfeit. Salmon and sea-bass swarm up the Dordogne and Garonne from here, whilst further up-river are *petites fritures* – small fry, crisped like whitebait. Everywhere trout, pike and eels are plentiful.

One of France's great joys are her trees: in Aquitaine these are as likely as not to be sweet chestnuts or walnuts – filling the *confiseries* with scrumptious cakes and sweets. Walnuts also make a *digestif* – but of course it shouldn't be mentioned in the same breath as 'the one' around here: Armagnac! The climate is kind to fruit and all around Agen is a gigantic orchard growing mainly plums. The world-famous *pruneaux d'Agen* are often stuffed with prune purée or other delights such as almond paste.

Aquitaine is a green and tranquil country, wearing its history gracefully to the eternal pleasure of its visitors.

AIL AU FOUR

Baked Garlic

A delicious starter or, served with bread and cheese and perhaps a little lettuce, it makes a good light meal. Take advantage of the few weeks – usually around June – when the fresh garlic is imported from France but don't attempt to prepare it with the dried garlic on sale during the rest of the year. Yes, unquestionably it does taste of garlic, but it's surprisingly mild!

Metric/Imperial
6 large bulbs fresh garlic
40 g/1½ oz butter (approximately)
salt
freshly ground black pepper

American
6 large bulbs fresh garlic
3 tablespoons butter (approximately)
salt
freshly ground black pepper

Ail au Four

Snip the long stalk from the garlic bulbs and cut a slice from the bottom to remove roots and provide a firm base. With a sharp pointed knife make a delicate incision all around the middle of each bulb and remove the papery skins above. Cut away some of the tougher skins around each clove and separate them from one another. Do not peel right down to the shiny centres of the cloves. Soften the butter and spread over the tops of the garlic bulbs.

Grease the bottom of an ovenproof dish, sprinkle generously with salt and

pepper and arrange the garlic bulbs in the dish. Cook uncovered in a preheated moderately hot oven (200°C/400°F/Gas Mark 6) for 30 minutes, then reduce the heat to moderate (160°C/325°F/Gas Mark 3), cover and bake for a further 1½ to 2 hours, depending on the size of the cloves. Test with a fine skewer to see if the garlic bulbs are tender. Serve with cream cheese, if liked.

SERVES 6

FICELLE DE BRANTOME

Stuffed Savoury Pancakes

Metric/Imperial
8 crêpes (see page 18)
225 g/8 oz cèpes or other mushrooms, sliced
15 g/½ oz butter
8 thin slices cooked ham
75 g/3 oz cheese, finely grated
200 ml/⅓ pint double cream, lightly whipped

American
8 crêpes (see page 18)
2 cups sliced cèpes or other mushrooms
1 tablespoon butter
8 thin slices processed ham
¾ cup finely grated cheese
1 cup heavy cream, lightly whipped

Make the *crêpes*. Sauté the *cèpes* or other mushrooms in the butter for 2 to 3 minutes.

Place a slice of ham on each pancake and top with the mushrooms. Roll up, arrange in an ovenproof serving dish and spoon the cream over. Sprinkle grated cheese on top and place under a preheated grill (broiler) until lightly browned and bubbling. Serve at once.

SERVES 4 OR 8

ESCALOPE DU BAR AUX CÈPES

Bass with Mushrooms

Metric/Imperial
1 bass, weighing about 2 kg/4½ lb
SAUCE:
1 small onion
1 small carrot
2 shallots
2 sprigs of fresh parsley
1 sprig of thyme
½ bay leaf
3 sage leaves
salt
freshly ground black pepper
1 litre/1¾ pints dry white wine
pinch of curry powder
150 ml/¼ pint double cream
4 egg yolks

2 × 15 ml spoons/2 tablespoons oil
2 oz/50 g butter
0.5 kg/1 lb cèpes or other mushrooms
6 × 15 ml spoons/6 tablespoons dry white wine
2 × 5 ml spoons/2 teaspoons grated onion
GARNISH:
few truffles, thinly sliced (optional)
fleurons (see page 44)

American
1 sea bass, weighing about 4½ lb
SAUCE:
1 small onion
1 small carrot
2 shallots
2 sprigs of fresh parsley
1 sprig of thyme
½ bay leaf
3 sage leaves
salt
freshly ground black pepper
4¼ cups dry white wine
pinch of curry powder
⅔ cup heavy cream
4 egg yolks

2 tablespoons oil
4 tablespoons butter
1 lb cèpes or other mushrooms
6 tablespoons dry white wine
2 teaspoons grated onion
GARNISH:
few truffles, thinly sliced (optional)
fleurons (see page 44)

Escalope du Bar aux Cèpes

Clean the fish and divide into 4 fillets, retaining trimmings. To make the sauce; place the vegetables, herbs, salt, pepper, wine and fish trimmings in a pan. Cover and simmer for 4 hours then strain. The liquid should measure about 250 ml/8 fl oz/1 cup; if necessary reduce to this quantity by boiling rapidly. Stir in the curry powder and all but 2 × 15 ml spoons/2 tablespoons of the cream and simmer gently for 30 minutes. Beat remaining cream and the egg yolks together; stir this liaison into the sauce and whisk in a bowl over hot water until the sauce thickens.

Heat the oil and half the butter in a sauté pan and fry the fish fillets until lightly browned on both sides. Season lightly, cover and leave the fish to cook in its own steam over very low heat until just tender.

Sauté the mushrooms in the remaining butter until lightly coloured. Add the wine and onion; simmer, uncovered, for 2 minutes.

Divide the mushrooms between 4 serving dishes and place the fish fillets on top. Garnish with truffle slices if used and *fleurons*, cut into decorative fish shapes. Boiled potatoes and fine *julienne* strips of leek, turnip, carrot and celery – cooked in equal quantities of red wine vinegar and water until tender – may be served as accompaniments.

SERVES 4

PETITS ROUGETS DU BASSIN AU CERFEUIL

Baked Red Mullet with Chervil

M. Darroze prefers the mullet he uses for this dish, which come from the nearby Arcachon Basin, to be tiny – 10–12 cm/4–5 inches long. He insists they should never be more than 18–20 cm/7–8 inches long, as the extra cooking required for larger fish alters the character of the dish.

Metric/Imperial
TOMATE CONCASSÉE:
15 g/½ oz butter
1 shallot, grated
100 g/4 oz tomatoes, skinned, seeded and chopped
1 small clove garlic, crushed
pinch of dried thyme
1 bay leaf
pinch of sugar

8–16 small red mullet, cleaned
salt
freshly ground black pepper
100 g/4 oz butter
2 × 15 ml spoons/2 tablespoons chopped fresh chervil

American
TOMATE CONCASSÉE:
1 tablespoon butter
1 shallot, grated
½ cup skinned, seeded and chopped tomatoes
1 small clove garlic, crushed
pinch of dried thyme
1 bay leaf
pinch of sugar

8–16 small red mullet or ocean perch, cleaned
salt
freshly ground black pepper
½ cup butter
2 tablespoons chopped fresh chervil

For the *tomate concassée*; melt the butter in a small pan and sauté the shallot for 2 to 3 minutes. Add the rest of the ingredients and simmer uncovered for about 15 minutes.

Arrange the cleaned fish in an oven-proof serving dish and season with salt and pepper. Spoon the tomato mixture over the fish and dot with the butter. Bake in a preheated hot oven (220°C/425°F/Gas Mark 7) for 4 to 5 minutes for tiny mullet, 8 to 10 minutes for slightly larger fish. Do not overcook.

Stir the chervil into the tomato mixture and serve immediately.
SERVES 4

SALADE DE MOULES AUX HERBES

Mussels with Herb Sauce

This delicious starter is a favourite throughout Aquitaine where fresh mussels are plentiful.

Metric/Imperial
2 kg/4–4½ lb small mussels
300 ml/½ pint dry white wine
SAUCE:
150 ml/¼ pint mayonnaise (see page 58 – ½ quantity)
2 × 15 ml spoons/2 tablespoons double cream
1–2 × 5 ml spoons/1–2 teaspoons tomato ketchup
1 × 15 ml spoon/1 tablespoon chopped fresh parsley
1 × 15 ml spoon/1 tablespoon chopped fresh chives
1 × 5 ml spoon/1 teaspoon chopped fresh chervil (optional)
1 × 5 ml spoon/1 teaspoon chopped fresh tarragon (optional)
few drops of white wine vinegar or lemon juice (optional)

American
4–4½ lb small mussels
1¼ cups dry white wine
SAUCE:
⅔ cup mayonnaise (see page 58 – ½ quantity)
2 tablespoons heavy cream
1–2 teaspoons tomato catsup
1 tablespoon chopped fresh parsley
1 tablespoon chopped fresh chives
1 teaspoon chopped fresh chervil (optional)
1 teaspoon chopped fresh tarragon (optional)
few drops of white wine vinegar or lemon juice (optional)

Scrub the mussels thoroughly in cold water and remove the beards. Discard any mussels with broken shells and any which do not close when given a sharp tap.

Put the mussels into a large, heavy-based pan and pour over the wine. Cover and cook over brisk heat until the shells open; about 5 minutes.

Remove the mussels from the pan, discard the empty top shells and arrange the mussels in their half shells in a serving dish. Allow to cool. Reserve the cooking liquor.

Prepare the mayonnaise and stir in the cream. Add 3–4 × 15 ml spoons/3–4 tablespoons of the reserved liquor and just enough tomato ketchup (catsup) to impart a faint blush. Stir in the chopped herbs. Add a few drops of vinegar, or

lemon juice if a sharper sauce is preferred, and a little more of the cooking liquor if required. The sauce should be thick enough to coat the back of a spoon.

Coat the mussels with the sauce just before serving.
SERVES 4

TRUITE AUX HERBES

Baked Stuffed Trout

Metric/Imperial
4 trout
STUFFING:
1 shallot, finely chopped
1 × 15 ml spoon/1 tablespoon chopped fresh tarragon
1 × 5 ml spoon/1 teaspoon dried thyme
2–3 × 15 ml spoons/2–3 tablespoons chopped fresh parsley
4 × 15 ml spoons/4 tablespoons breadcrumbs
salt
freshly ground black pepper
2 × 5 ml spoons/2 teaspoons oil (approximately)

150 ml/¼ pint dry white wine

American
4 trout
STUFFING:
1 shallot, finely chopped
1 tablespoon chopped fresh tarragon
1 teaspoon dried thyme
2–3 tablespoons chopped fresh parsley
4 tablespoons bread crumbs
salt
freshly ground black pepper
2 teaspoons oil (approximately)

⅔ cup dry white wine

Wash and clean the trout and dry thoroughly. Mix the shallot, herbs and breadcrumbs together. Season with salt and pepper and bind the stuffing with oil. Divide equally into 4 portions and stuff the trout.

Place the trout in an oiled ovenproof dish. Sprinkle with salt and pepper and moisten with the wine. Cook in a pre-heated hot oven (220°C/425°F/Gas Mark 7) for about 8 minutes or until fish are just cooked.

Serve the trout with the cooking juices spooned over.
SERVES 4

Petits Rougets du Bassin au Cerfeuil,
Salade de Moules aux Herbes

PIÈCE DE BOEUF MARINÉE, SAUCE CHEVREUIL

Fillet Steak in Rich Sauce

Metric/Imperial

1 fillet of beef, weighing about 2 kg/4½ lb
MARINADE:
1 onion, sliced
1 clove garlic, crushed
4 sprigs of parsley
½ bay leaf
1 sprig of thyme
8 peppercorns, lightly crushed
generous pinch of coarse sea salt
8 juniper berries, lightly crushed
2 cloves
1 bottle red Bordeaux or other red wine

Espagnole sauce (see recipe)
2 × 15 ml spoons/2 tablespoons raspberry or redcurrant jelly
100 g/4 oz truffles or flat mushrooms, finely diced
salt
freshly ground black pepper

American

1 filet of beef, weighing about 4½ lb
MARINADE:
1 onion, sliced
1 clove garlic, crushed
4 sprigs of parsley
½ bay leaf
1 sprig of thyme
8 peppercorns, lightly crushed
generous pinch of coarse sea salt
8 juniper berries, lightly crushed
2 cloves
1 bottle red Bordeaux or other red wine

Espagnole sauce (see recipe)
2 tablespoons raspberry or redcurrant jelly
1 cup finely diced truffles or flat mushrooms
salt
freshly ground black pepper

Trim the meat, removing all traces of fat and gristle. Place the whole fillet in a bowl with the marinade ingredients, cover and leave to marinate in a cool place for 48 hours; turn the meat once or twice.

Prepare the Espagnole sauce according to the recipe given for *Caneton à la Bigarade* (page 46). Lift meat out of the marinade. Strain the marinade into a pan and add an equal quantity of Espagnole sauce. Simmer, covered, as gently as possible for 4 hours. Strain finely. Add the jelly and truffles or mushrooms and simmer for 30 minutes. Check seasoning and texture; the sauce should be a thick pouring consistency – if too thin, reduce further by simmering uncovered.

Dry the fillet in a cloth and cut into 8 thick tournedo steaks. Dust lightly with salt and pepper and cook quickly under a preheated very hot grill (broiler) for 5 to 10 minutes, turning once.

Arrange on a warm serving dish and coat liberally with sauce. Serve with puréed chestnuts, puréed carrots, sautéed *cèpes* or mushrooms and fried cucumber strips. For the purées, boil the chestnuts and carrots separately in salted water until tender; drain, (shell the chestnuts) and pass through a sieve (strainer) or vegetable mill. Moisten the chestnut purée with milk. Season both purées.
SERVES 8

LA MIQUE DU SARLADAIS

Pot-au-Feu with Dumplings

Recognizing that even the most devoted gourmet may tire of *foie gras* and truffles, Michel Garrigou has a summer programme of *menus de grand-mère* at Hotel St-Albert so that those interested in 'real' provincial cooking can enjoy traditional old Périgordian dishes.

Metric/Imperial

1.5 kg/3½ lb salt spare ribs of pork
2.75 litres/5 pints stock
1.5 kg/3½ lb vegetables (potatoes, leeks, carrots, turnips, celeriac etc.)
1 large onion, studded with 2 cloves
freshly ground black pepper
salt
MIQUE:
225 g/8 oz stale bread, finely diced
15 g/½ oz fresh yeast
3 eggs, beaten
3 × 15 ml spoons/3 tablespoons oil
75 g/3 oz bacon, finely chopped

American

3–3½ lb salt spareribs of pork
6 pints stock
3–3½ lb vegetables (potatoes, leeks, carrots, turnips, celeriac etc.)
1 large onion, studded with 2 cloves
freshly ground black pepper
salt
MIQUE:
½ lb stale bread, finely diced
½ cake compressed yeast
3 eggs, beaten
3 tablespoons oil
⅓ cup finely chopped bacon

Place the meat and stock in a large pan. Bring slowly to the boil, skim, then simmer for 30 minutes. Cut the vegetables into chunks. Add to the pan and season with pepper, and salt if necessary. Simmer for about 45 minutes.

To prepare the *mique*; place bread in a bowl and moisten with a little of the stock. Blend yeast with 1 × 5 ml spoon/1 teaspoon warm water. Work the yeast into the bread together with the eggs, oil, bacon and seasoning; adding a little more stock if necessary to give a manageable dough. Form into an oval shape and leave in a warm place for 45 minutes.

When the vegetables are cooked, transfer them to a warm serving dish and keep hot. Carefully slide the *mique* into the stock and simmer for 30 minutes.

Lift the *mique* onto a serving dish. Cut the meat into serving pieces and arrange around the *mique* with the vegetables. Strain some of the stock into a sauceboat and serve gherkins (sweet dill pickles) as an accompaniment.
SERVES 6 TO 8

Salade Périgordine (below)

La Mique du Sarladais (above)

SALADE PÉRIGORDINE

Périgord Salad

Metric/Imperial
1 lettuce
4–6 tomatoes, cut into wedges
4 hard-boiled eggs, chopped
8–12 walnuts, roughly chopped
3 thick slices streaky bacon, cut into strips
FRENCH DRESSING:
1.5 × 15 ml spoons/1½ tablespoons wine vinegar
1 × 5 ml spoon/1 teaspoon lemon juice
5 × 15 ml spoons/5 tablespoons walnut, sunflower or corn oil
1 × 2.5 ml spoon/½ teaspoon sugar
1 × 2.5 ml spoon/½ teaspoon French mustard
1 clove garlic, crushed
salt
freshly ground black pepper

American
1 lettuce
4–6 tomatoes, cut into wedges
4 hard-cooked eggs, chopped
8–12 walnuts, roughly chopped
3 thick slices bacon, cut into strips
FRENCH DRESSING:
1½ tablespoons wine vinegar
1 teaspoon lemon juice
5 tablespoons walnut, sunflower or corn oil
½ teaspoon sugar
½ teaspoon French mustard
1 clove garlic, crushed
salt
freshly ground black pepper

Place the lettuce leaves, tomato wedges, chopped eggs, and walnuts in a large salad bowl and mix well. Fry the bacon without extra fat, over moderate heat until crisp.

To make the dressing; shake all the ingredients together in a screw-top jar. To serve, add the dressing to the salad and toss thoroughly. Stir in the hot bacon pieces and serve immediately.
SERVES 4

TOURTIÈRE DE POULET AU SALSIFIS

Chicken and Salsify Pie

At Hotel Bonnet, they used an antique copper pan as a pie mould and baked a facsimile of the lid as well, but this is equally delicious baked in a pie-dish in traditional fashion.

Metric/Imperial

pâte brisée (see recipe)
50 g/2 oz cooking fat
1 chicken, weighing about 1.5 kg/ 3–3½ lb, quartered
750 g/1½ lb salsify, cut into 2.5 cm/1 inch pieces
1 × 15 ml spoon/1 tablespoon flour
1 clove garlic, crushed
300 ml/½ pint chicken stock
1 × 15 ml spoon/1 tablespoon chopped fresh parsley
salt
freshly ground black pepper

American

pâte brisée (see recipe)
¼ cup cooking fat
1 chicken, weighing about 3–3½ lb, quartered
1½ lb salsify, cut into 1 inch pieces
1 tablespoon flour
1 clove garlic, crushed
1¼ cups chicken stock
1 tablespoon chopped fresh parsley
salt
freshly ground black pepper

Prepare the *pâte brisée* according to the recipe given for *Tarte à l'Oignon* (page 79); chill. Heat the fat in a large pan and seal the chicken pieces over moderate heat. Add the salsify and sauté lightly. Take out the chicken and salsify.

Sprinkle the flour and garlic into the pan, then gradually blend in the stock. Replace the chicken and salsify and add the parsley, salt and pepper. Cover and simmer for 20 minutes; cool until luke-warm.

Skim the stock. Take out the chicken and remove the skin and bones; cut the meat into serving pieces. Place a layer of chicken in a 1.5 litre/2½ pint pie-dish. Cover with a layer of salsify. Continue these layers and finally add any remaining cooking liquor.

Roll out the pastry to a circle large enough to cover the pie-dish. Damp edges of pie-dish and place pastry lid over the filling. Trim and make a few slits in the centre. Decorate the top with pastry leaves, cut from the trimmings. Bake in a preheated moderately hot oven (200°C/ 400°F/Gas Mark 6) for 30 to 35 minutes. Serve hot.
SERVES 4 TO 6

FLAN AUX POIRES ET AUX NOIX

Pear and Walnut Flan

Metric/Imperial

pâte sucrée (see recipe)
225 g/8 oz shelled walnut halves
2–3 dessert pears, peeled, cored and sliced
300 ml/½ pint milk
1 egg
1 egg yolk
1 × 15 ml spoon/1 tablespoon sugar
2 × 15 ml spoons/2 tablespoons kirsch or pear brandy

American

pâte sucrée (see recipe)
2 cups shelled walnut halves
2–3 dessert pears, peeled, cored and sliced
1¼ cups milk
1 egg
1 egg yolk
1 tablespoon sugar
2 tablespoons kirsch or pear brandy

Make the *pâte sucrée* according to the recipe given for *Tarte Normande* (page 20), using half quantities. After resting, roll out the pastry thinly and use to line a 20 cm/8 inch flan ring set on a baking sheet. Chill for 15 minutes.

Line the base of the flan with the wal-nuts, reserving some for decoration. Cover with the pears. Bring the milk almost to the boil. Beat the egg, egg yolk, sugar and liqueur in a bowl. Pour the milk onto the eggs, beating well. Strain the custard into the flan and bake in a preheated moder-ately hot oven (200°C/400°F/Gas Mark 6) for 10 minutes. Reduce the temperature to moderate (180°C/350°F/Gas Mark 4) and bake for a further 20 to 30 minutes until custard has set and pastry is golden.

Remove the flan ring and decorate with the reserved walnuts. Serve warm or cold.
SERVES 6

Tourtière de Poulet au Salsifis, Flan aux Poires et aux Noix

TOURTIÈRE BONAGUIL

Flaky Tipsy Fruit Tart

Metric/Imperial
0.5 kg/1 lb apples or pears
small glass of rum
PÂTE À LA VIENNOISE:
225 g/8 oz plain flour
4 × 15 ml spoons/4 tablespoons corn oil
4 × 15 ml spoons/4 tablespoons warm
   water (approximately)
oil for brushing
sugar for sprinkling

American
1 lb apples or pears
small glass of rum
PÂTE À LA VIENNOISE:
2 cups all-purpose flour
4 tablespoons corn oil
4 tablespoons warm water
   (approximately)
oil for brushing
sugar for sprinkling

Peel, core and slice the fruit; soak in the rum for at least 1 hour.

For the *pâte*; sift flour into a bowl, make a well in the centre and stir in the oil and water. Work to a soft dough, adding more water if necessary. Knead thoroughly on a lightly floured surface then roll out to a long strip, about 5 cm/ 2 inches thick. Lift one end of the dough, stretch and hit it hard against the working surface. Repeat, lifting alternate ends of the dough, for 10 minutes. Cover and rest for 30 minutes.

Drain the fruit. Roll out one-quarter pastry as thinly as possible. Brush with a little oil. Working on a small area at a time, carefully stretch the dough over the hands until it is paper-thin and almost transparent. Cut out rounds of pastry, about 20 cm/8 inches in diameter. Place these layers on top of each other on a lightly greased baking sheet. Cover with a layer of fruit.

Roll out another quarter of dough and cut out layers as before. Place over the fruit, then arrange the remaining fruit on top. Cover with pastry layers, cut from another quarter of dough. Roll out remaining dough thinly and cut into strips, curl these and brush with oil. Arrange in a decorative pattern on top of the tart. Sprinkle with sugar. Bake in a preheated hot oven (220°C/425°F/Gas Mark 7) for 10 minutes. Lower the heat to (200°C/ 400°F/Gas Mark 6) and bake for about 30 minutes until crisp and golden brown. Serve hot or cold.
SERVES 4 TO 6

Tourtière Bonaguil (above right); Village market in Périgord (right)

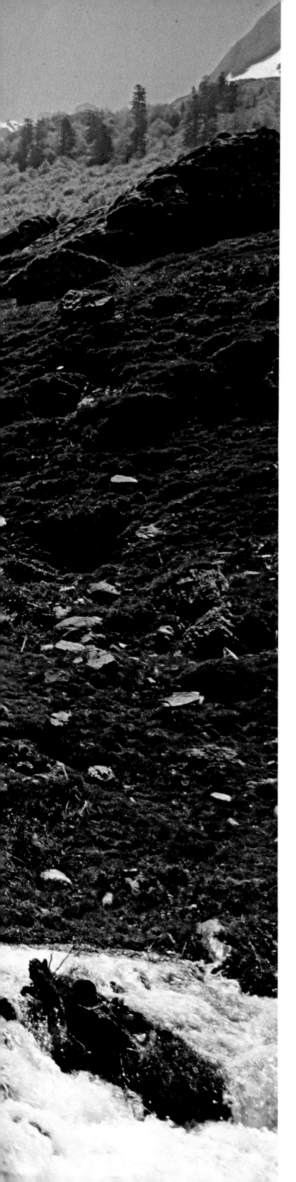

Pyrenees: Navarre, Béarn, Bigorre, Roussillon

This chapter's area is more diverse than most, ranging from the haughty grandeur of the Pyrenean peaks to the sweltering fruit-bowl of Roussillon, with a quite different sea at each end. The Edwardian elegance of Biarritz contrasts with the Castillet in Perpignan. The Biscay port of St-Jean-de-Luz is totally unlike the eastern Collioure, where smaller boats catch anchovies and exotic-looking Mediterranean fish. Big four-square Basque houses with bold reddish balconies and shutters, carrying their birthdate and first owners' names on the lintel, give way to low crouching mountain buildings before descending to the warm ochre tiles of Roussillon. To the north soar the towering walls and battlements of the fortified city of Carcassonne. In the southern valleys are attenuated spa towns where people still 'take the cure'.

Unifying all is the proximity of Spain. Navarre straddled the present border in the west and the people are Basques, neither French nor Spanish or perhaps both. In the east the influence is Catalonian, as exemplified in the Kings of Majorca's Palace in Perpignan. The food has a strong Spanish flavour with tomatoes and peppers in abundance. Bayonne is famous for chocolate, which came from Spain in the 17th Century, as well as for outstanding ham. Beans are ubiquitous: the great *cassoulets* of Castelnaudary and elsewhere: the many *garbures* (thick bean soups) mutating into *ouillades* as you travel eastwards. Multifarious fish soups are prevalent near the two coastlines. Game is plentiful, especially birds, with pigeons the main autumn target. To drink: spicy golden Jurançon in Navarre, robust red Madiran from Béarn, fortified sweet apéritifs and dessert wines near the south-east coast and strong fruity ones from Corbières.

Pollarded planes are as prevalent as in the Midi, for these southern summers are hot. Nevertheless a couple of hours' drive can take you from tropical lilies and date-palms, through English garden roses and geraniums, to tiny alpine flowers. In springtime, when these are at their best, you will also find snow and may be lucky to sight some izard. You'll certainly see fork-tailed kites and probably eagles, perhaps even lammergeyers.

Excellent roads carry you safely and spectacularly east-west: from the hot flat Mediterranean littoral, past long-ruined castles on bare peaks standing in poignant memorial to the massacres of the Albigensian wars; past Vauban's 'forgotten' fortress-town of Mont-Louis and through the historic Comté de Foix, where they used to pan for gold in the Middle Ages. Past Bernadette's shrine at Lourdes, on to St-Jean-Pied-de Port with its pretty old town beneath yet another fortress; through the green Basque hills and at last to the Bay of Biscay. But it's the north-south roads which really seduce. These twist and climb through the valleys alongside hurtling streams, milky with snow-water or glittering as gin-and-tonic, and through small hard-working villages. Most are aiming for an ultimate col which may lead to Spain or (officially at least!) may not. Some finish in awe-inspiring rocky amphitheatres, like the cliff-ringed Cirque de Gavarnie. All have their own special delights.

GARBURE BLANCHE

Thick Bean Soup

Begin preparing this one-dish meal the day before you intend to eat it. Although categorized as a soup, this *Béarnais garbure* should be 'thick' enough to support a ladle. It is substantial enough to be served as a main course.

The beans used were once *haricot mais*, which grew amongst the maize, but are now more often *langots plats*, which may be bought in local markets; haricot (navy) beans or butter beans are suitable equivalents.

Metric/Imperial
250 g/9 oz haricot beans or butter beans, soaked overnight in cold water
6–8 salted pork spare ribs
1 ham bone
large handful of chopped ham rind or bacon rind
6 large potatoes, roughly chopped
salt
2 large onions, chopped
50 g/2 oz goose or pork fat
1 cabbage, weighing about 1.5 kg/ 3–3½ lb
freshly ground black pepper

Garbure Blanche

American
1–1¼ cups navy beans or butter beans, soaked overnight in cold water
6–8 salted pork spareribs
1 ham bone
large handful of chopped ham rind or bacon rind
6 large potatoes, roughly chopped
salt
2 large onions, chopped
¼ cup goose or pork fat
1 cabbage, weighing about 3–3½ lb
freshly ground black pepper

Drain the beans and put them with the meat, bone and rind in a large saucepan. Cover with water and bring to the boil. Lower the heat and simmer gently for 5 hours, stirring and skimming occasionally. Leave, covered, in a cool place overnight.

Next day, cook the potatoes in boiling salted water for 15 minutes; drain. Sauté the onions in the fat until softened. Skim the *garbure*, add the potatoes and onions and simmer for 1 hour. Cook the cabbage separately in boiling salted water until tender; drain.

Before serving, season the *garbure* with pepper, and salt if necessary. Take out the ham bone. Place a generous spoonful of cabbage in each warmed soup bowl. Spoon over the *garbure*, dividing the meat equally between the bowls.
SERVES 6 TO 8

PIPERADE

Metric/Imperial
25 g/1 oz butter
4 × 15 ml spoons/4 tablespoons oil
400 g/14 oz onions, finely chopped
0.5 kg/1 lb green peppers, cored, seeded, and roughly chopped
1 kg/2 lb tomatoes, peeled, seeded and chopped
3 cloves garlic, crushed
bouquet garni
salt
freshly ground black pepper
4 thin slices Bayonne or other raw ham or gammon
4 eggs, lightly beaten
chopped fresh parsley to garnish

American
2 tablespoons butter
4 tablespoons oil
3½ cups finely chopped onions
1 lb green peppers, cored, seeded and roughly chopped
2 lb tomatoes, peeled, seeded and chopped
3 cloves garlic
bouquet garni
salt
freshly ground black pepper

Piperade, Truite Labourdine, Pintade aux Prunes Fraîches (page 36)

4 thin slices Bayonne or other uncooked
   ham
4 eggs, lightly beaten
chopped fresh parsley to garnish

Heat the butter and half of the oil in a frying pan (skillet) and sauté the onions until they begin to soften. Add the peppers and cook for 2 to 3 minutes. Stir in the tomatoes, garlic, bouquet garni, salt and pepper. Simmer gently for 30 minutes.

Fry the ham in the remaining oil until tender. Keep warm. Remove vegetable mixture from the heat, discard the bouquet garni, and slowly pour in the beaten eggs, stirring briskly. Return to a low heat, stir until the mixture is slightly thick and creamy.

Place the ham on top; serve hot garnished with chopped parsley.

SERVES 4 TO 6

TRUITE LABOURDINE

Trout with Ham

Metric/Imperial
4 trout, each weighing about 225 g/8 oz,
   cleaned
4 large thin slices Bayonne or other raw
   ham or gammon
oil for shallow frying
freshly ground black pepper
4 cloves garlic, finely chopped
2 large handfuls of chopped fresh
   parsley
1–2 × 15 ml spoons/1–2 tablespoons
   wine vinegar

American
4 trout, each weighing about ½ lb,
   cleaned
4 large thin slices Bayonne or other
   uncooked ham
oil for shallow frying

freshly ground black pepper
4 cloves garlic, finely chopped
2 large handfuls of chopped fresh
   parsley
1–2 tablespoons wine vinegar

Wrap each trout in a slice of ham. Heat the oil in a large frying pan (skillet) and fry the trout for about 3 minutes. Take off heat, remove the ham and cut it into strips.

Return trout to pan, season with pepper and cook over low heat for about 2 minutes on each side, basting continuously. Add the ham and cook for a further 4 minutes, turning the fish once. Place the ham in a hot serving dish and arrange the fish on top. Keep warm.

Pour off most of the oil from the pan, add the garlic and cook until just beginning to brown. Sprinkle in the parsley and vinegar and stir over low heat for 1 to 2 minutes. Arrange this mixture over the trout and serve at once.

SERVES 4

Make a *mirepoix* by sweating the carrots and onions in two-thirds of the butter until softened. Simmer the plums in the wine, adding sugar to taste, until tender. Drain, reserving the liquor; keep the plums warm.

Season the guinea fowl portions with salt and pepper. Heat the oil in a deep sauté pan and brown the bird slowly. Add the *mirepoix*, plum liquor and bouquet garni. Simmer for 30 minutes or until the bird is tender.

Transfer the guinea fowl to a warmed serving dish, add the plums and keep hot. Strain the cooking liquor into a small pan. Blend remaining butter with the flour. Whisk this *beurre manié* into the liquor, a little at a time, over gentle heat. Cook, stirring, until the sauce is thick and glossy. Pour over the guinea fowl and plums

SERVES 4

PAELLA À MON FACON

Basque-Style Paella

The Basque country bestrides the Pyrenees into both France and Spain sharing a culture not only of language, dress and dance, but also of cooking. Thus it is no surprise to find paella as a *spécialité de la maison* on the French side of the border.

Saffron gives paella its traditional golden colour. If you do not have any substitute turmeric to obtain the same colour effect and a pleasant, but weaker flavour.

Metric/Imperial
1.5 kg/3–3½ lb mussels
25 clams or cockles
300 ml/½ pint dry white wine
1 chicken, weighing about 1.25 kg/2½ lb, cut into serving pieces
4–5 × 15 ml spoons/4–5 tablespoons olive oil
1 large onion, chopped
1 large red pepper, cored, seeded and diced
1 large green pepper, cored, seeded and diced
225 g/8 oz chorizo sausage, thickly sliced
225 g/8 oz Bayonne or other raw ham, diced
350 g/12 oz filleted hake, cut into chunks
250 g/9 oz long-grain rice
1 × 2.5 ml spoon/½ teaspoon saffron
salt
freshly ground black pepper
300 ml/½ pint chicken stock
225 g/8 oz roasted pork, diced
GARNISH:
8 live Dublin Bay prawns or crayfish (optional)
chopped fresh parsley

PINTADE AUX PRUNES FRAÎCHES

Poulet Sauté à la Basquaise

Guinea Fowl with Plums

Metric/Imperial
225 g/8 oz carrots, chopped
100 g/4 oz onions, chopped
75 g/3 oz butter
1 kg/2 lb plums
300 ml/½ pint white wine
sugar to taste
1 guinea fowl, weighing about 1.5 kg/ 3–3½ lb, jointed
salt
freshly ground black pepper
3 × 15 ml spoons/3 tablespoons oil
bouquet garni
25 g/1 oz flour

American
2 cups chopped carrots
1 cup chopped onions
⅓ cup butter
2 lb plums
1¼ cups white wine
sugar to taste
1 guinea fowl, weighing about 3–3½ lb, quartered
salt
freshly ground black pepper
3 tablespoons oil
bouquet garni
¼ cup flour

American
3–3½ lb mussels
25 clams
1¼ cups dry white wine
1 chicken, weighing about 2½ lb, cut
 into serving pieces
4–5 tablespoons olive oil
1 large onion, chopped
1 large red pepper, cored, seeded and
 diced
1 large green pepper, cored, seeded and
 diced
½ lb chorizo sausage, thickly sliced
½ lb Bayonne or other uncooked ham
¾ lb fileted hake, cut into chunks
1⅓ cups long-grain rice
½ teaspoon saffron
salt
freshly ground black pepper
1¼ cups chicken stock
½ lb roasted pork, diced
GARNISH:
8 live jumbo shrimp or écrevisses
 (optional)
chopped fresh parsley

Scrub the mussels and clams or cockles thoroughly in cold water, discarding any with open shells. Place in a pan with the wine and an equal quantity of water. Cover and cook over brisk heat for 5 minutes. Drain, reserving the liquor.

Sauté the chicken pieces in the oil in a large sauté pan. Add the onion and peppers; cook, stirring, until they begin to soften. Stir in the sausage, ham and hake and cook for a few minutes. Shower in the rice and stir-fry for 2 minutes. Sprinkle in the saffron, salt and pepper.

Pour in the stock with the reserved cooking liquor; adding a little water, if necessary, to ensure the liquid just covers the ingredients. Cover and simmer for 15 to 20 minutes or until the rice is just tender and the liquid has been absorbed.

Meanwhile, if garnishing with whole shellfish, plunge these into boiling water and cook rapidly until bright red; 10 to 15 minutes.

Lightly mix the mussels, clams or cockles, and pork into the paella. Garnish with the whole shellfish, if used, and sprinkle with chopped parsley.
SERVES 8

POULET SAUTÉ À LA BASQUAISE

Basque-Style Chicken

This traditional Basque dish of chicken with tomatoes and peppers should ideally include 1 or 2 *piments basques* – spicy peppers resembling chillies but less hot. If unobtainable, a chilli pepper may be used instead of one of the green peppers, if liked.

Metric/Imperial
1 spring chicken, weighing about
 1.25 kg/2½ lb
salt
freshly ground black pepper
flour for coating
6 × 15 ml spoons/6 tablespoons oil
4 onions, finely chopped
2 green peppers, cored, seeded and sliced
2 red peppers, cored, seeded and sliced
4 cloves garlic, crushed with a little oil
0.5 kg/1 lb tomatoes, skinned, seeded
 and roughly chopped
2 × 15 ml spoons/2 tablespoons tomato
 purée
bouquet garni (thyme, bay, parsley,
 chervil)
175 g/6 oz piece of Bayonne or other
 raw ham
cayenne pepper to taste
chopped fresh parsley to garnish

American
1 broiler-fryer chicken, weighing about
 2½ lb
salt
freshly ground black pepper
flour for coating
6 tablespoons oil
4 onions, finely chopped
2 green peppers, cored, seeded and sliced
2 red peppers, cored, seeded and sliced
4 cloves garlic, crushed with a little oil
1 lb tomatoes, skinned, seeded and
 roughly chopped
2 tablespoons tomato paste
bouquet garni (thyme, bay, parsley,
 chervil)
6 oz piece of Bayonne or other uncooked
 ham
cayenne pepper to taste
chopped fresh parsley to garnish

Divide the chicken into 4 portions, removing excess fat and skin. Dust the pieces with seasoned flour. Heat 4 × 15 ml spoons/4 tablespoons of the oil in a sauté pan and fry the chicken over brisk heat until golden brown all over. Lower the heat, cover and cook for 10 minutes. Take out the chicken pieces.

Add the remaining oil to the pan and sauté the onions for 2 to 3 minutes. Add the peppers, garlic, tomatoes, tomato purée (paste), bouquet garni and ham. Moisten with a little water and check the seasoning, adding cayenne pepper and salt to taste. Cover and cook for 15 minutes. Replace the chicken pieces in the pan and simmer, covered, for 30 to 35 minutes or until the chicken is tender.

Discard the bouquet garni and dice the ham. Sprinkle with chopped parsley and serve with boiled rice.
SERVES 4

Paella à mon Façon

SÁUTE D'AGNEAU À LA NAVARRAISE

Navarre-Style Lamb

This succulent dish was prepared for us by M. Arcé, whose Basque cooking has been rewarded with a Michelin star.

Metric/Imperial
1 kg/2 lb boned leg of lamb
salt
freshly ground black pepper
25 g/1 oz butter
4 × 15 ml spoons/4 tablespoons oil
2 onions, finely chopped
1 × 15 ml spoon/1 tablespoon vinegar
3 red peppers, cored, seeded and sliced
1–2 cloves garlic, crushed
pinch of cayenne pepper
chopped fresh parsley to garnish

American
2 lb boned leg of lamb
salt
freshly ground black pepper
2 tablespoons butter
4 tablespoons oil
2 onions, finely chopped
1 tablespoon vinegar
3 red peppers, cored, seeded and sliced
1–2 cloves garlic, crushed
pinch of cayenne pepper
chopped fresh parsley to garnish

Cut the lamb into 2.5 cm/1 inch cubes and season with salt and pepper. Heat the butter and 2 × 15 ml spoons/2 tablespoons oil in a sauté pan over moderate heat and sauté the lamb until evenly browned. Add the onions, cover and cook gently for 10 minutes. Stir in the vinegar and leave, covered, to one side.

In a separate pan, sauté the peppers in the remaining oil for 2 to 3 minutes, stirring. Add the garlic, cover and cook gently for 5 minutes.

Add the peppers and garlic to the meat with the cayenne pepper and salt to taste. Cover and simmer gently for 10 minutes or until the meat is tender.

Arrange on a hot serving dish and sprinkle with chopped parsley.
SERVES 4 TO 6

TARTE AUX CERISES

Cherry Tart

Ceret snuggles in a secret valley between the hot plains of Roussillon and the Pyrennean grandeur and majesty. Though in full sight of Mont Canigou's eternal snows, the cherry orchards here ripen incredibly early; their fruit is often in the markets before the end of April.

Metric/Imperial
PÂTE:
250 g/9 oz flour
pinch of salt
75 g/3 oz sugar
15 g/½ oz fresh yeast, crumbled
2 eggs
100 g/4 oz butter, softened
cold water (as necessary)
FILLING:
25 g/1 oz cornflour
0.5 litre/18 fl oz warm milk
4 eggs
150 g/5 oz sugar
750 g/1½ lb cherries, stoned

American
PÂTE:
2¼ cups all-purpose flour
pinch of salt
⅓ cup sugar
½ cake compressed yeast, crumbled
2 eggs
½ cup softened butter
cold water (as necessary)
FILLING:
¼ cup cornstarch
2¼ cups warm milk
4 eggs
⅔ cup sugar
1½ lb cherries, pitted

Tarte aux Cerises

For the *pâte*; sift the flour and salt onto a working surface and mix in the sugar. Work the yeast thoroughly into the mixture. Make a well in the centre and add the eggs and butter. Draw the flour into the centre with the fingertips. Mix to a supple dough, adding a little water if necessary. Knead very lightly and leave, covered with a sheet of oiled polythene (plastic), at room temperature for 2 hours.

To prepare filling; blend the cornflour with a little of the milk. Beat in the eggs and sugar. Stir in the remaining warm milk, gradually. Pour into a saucepan and place over low heat. Cook gently, whisking constantly, until the custard thickens. Strain, if necessary to remove any lumps.

Roll out the pastry thinly and use it to line a 25 cm/10 inch flan ring placed on a greased baking sheet. Arrange the cherries in the flan and carefully pour in the cooled custard. Cook in a preheated moderately hot oven (190°C/375°F/Gas Mark 5) for 20 to 30 minutes or until the pastry is golden and the custard set. Serve warm or cold.
SERVES 10 TO 12

American

SORBET:
½ cup sugar
1¼ cups water
juice of ½ lemon
½ lb raspberries or strawberries
2 egg whites
COULIS:
½ cup sugar
6 tablespoons water
1 teaspoon unflavored gelatin
¾ lb raspberries, crushed

¼ lb strawberries
¼ lb raspberries
sugar to taste
¼ lb blackberries

For the sorbet; dissolve the sugar in the water over low heat then boil steadily for 10 minutes. Add the lemon juice and leave to cool. Sieve the fruit to a purée and stir into the cooled syrup. Pour into a suitable container and freeze until mushy. Whip the egg whites until stiff, then fold into the fruit mixture and freeze until firm.

To prepare the *coulis*; dissolve the sugar in the water over low heat then boil steadily for 10 minutes. Dissolve the gelatine in 1 × 15 ml spoon/1 tablespoon warm water, then stir into the syrup. Pour over the crushed raspberries and mix thoroughly. Cool slightly then sieve and chill.

To serve; scoop the sorbet into individual serving dishes. Divide the strawberries and raspberries evenly between the dishes; sprinkle with sugar to taste. Pour the *coulis* over the fruit and top with the blackberries.
SERVES 6

COUPE MARTUXA

Raspberry Sundae

Martuxa is Basque for both *framboise* (raspberry) and *mûre* (blackberry). This simple iced dessert can be made with any mixture of fresh or frozen soft red fruits, the more the merrier!

Metric/Imperial
SORBET:
100 g/4 oz sugar
300 ml/½ pint water
juice of ½ lemon
225 g/8 oz raspberries or strawberries
2 egg whites
COULIS:
100 g/4 oz sugar
6 × 15 ml spoons/6 tablespoons water
1 × 5 ml spoon/1 teaspoon gelatine
325 g/12 oz raspberries, crushed

100 g/4 oz strawberries
100 g/4 oz raspberries
sugar to taste
100 g/4 oz blackberries

Shepherd with his Béarnais sheep in the Pyrenees

Perche, Île-de-France, Berry, Nivernais

This chapter briefly touches on four lightly-connected regions loosely strung around the shoulders of Paris. Perche, the westernmost province of the group, is best known for its heavy horses, the chunky Percherons. Except for the lack of coastline it closely resembles neighbouring Normandie. Within easy reach of the capital, even before modern transportation the whole area was popular for country-house building on a lavish scale. Large and beautiful houses and *châteaux* are set in a smiling countryside and many pretty villages have been lovingly preserved by well-to-do weekenders and commuters. This nearness to Paris also means that there are lots of excellent places to eat and stay – many at prices well below what you might expect.

Livestock, vegetables and fruit flourish, and this richness is reflected *à la table*. Cause for local pride are *champignons de Paris* (button mushrooms), Berrichone lambs, salmon-trout, bream and a variety of other fish including eels; also, perhaps surprisingly in what is almost the suburbs of Paris, game. The cheeses are superb and most subtle, such as Brie. Berry, particularly, has a sweet tooth with a multitude of specialities in the cake line and a visit to a good pâtisserie in Bourges is an education. The famous 'upside-down' *tarte Tatin* comes from this region. With the celebrated vineyards of Touraine to the west and Chablis to the east, the only well known wines from hereabouts are those clean flinty whites from the upper Loire, Sancerre and Pouilly Fumé. These attractive villages produce red wines too, and there are many other likeable vintages produced, and best drunk, within the region.

Nivernais was a sometime part of Bourgogne; its hills are choppier and its soil chalkier, which is why its famous crisp wine – Chablis, has almost as much in common with its northern neighbour – Champagne, as with the rounder wines of Burgundy. Its capital is Avallon, a town as attractive as its name and boasting an exceptionally pretty hotel, the Poste. Vauban, whose mighty 17th Century fortifications are found all over France, is commemorated here. His statue stands in a square bustling with day-by-day activity, while the old walled town takes life with a quieter dignity. Try not to miss nearby Vezelay, where the great basilica of Notre-Dame rises on the high brow of a hill. Visible from afar, which must have been an advantage to medieval pilgrims, it was one of the starting points of the pilgrimages to St-Jacques-de-Compostelle. Its huge naves and aisles testify to the enormous concourse of penitents who gathered here to be blessed before they set out on their 750-mile walk to western Spain. Though inevitably much restored, its vast doors, soaring columns and prolific carvings are a moving reminder of an earlier faith.

TERRINE DE PETITS LÉGUMES FRAIS

Fresh Vegetable Terrine

The vegetables given below are those M. Meneau recommended when he made this terrine in late May but any tender, non-watery vegetables in season can be used instead. The stock should be highly-flavoured; ideally use jellied chicken stock (see page 94) and reduce the quantity of gelatine to 1 × 5 ml spoon/1 teaspoon.

Metric/Imperial
2 bunches of radishes, trimmed and
    peeled
large bunch of fresh parsley, chopped
freshly ground green or white pepper
    (optional)
0.5 kg/1 lb asparagus, chopped
350 g/12 oz young carrots, chopped
350 g/12 oz young turnips, chopped
1 litre/1¾ pints chicken stock
2 avocados, peeled, stoned and chopped
5 × 5 ml spoons/5 teaspoons gelatine
SAUCE:
½ avocado, peeled
1 large tomato, skinned, seeded and
    chopped
1–2 × 5 ml spoons/1–2 teaspoons each
    chopped fresh chervil, chives and
    tarragon
250 ml/8 fl oz olive oil
pinch of ground coriander

American
2 bunches of radishes, trimmed and
    peeled
large bunch of fresh parsley, chopped
freshly ground green or white pepper
    (optional)
1 lb asparagus, chopped
¾ lb young carrots, chopped
¾ lb young turnips, chopped
4¼ cups chicken stock
2 avocados, peeled, pitted and chopped
5 teaspoons unflavored gelatin
SAUCE:
½ avocado, peeled
1 large tomato, skinned, seeded and
    chopped
1–2 teaspoons each chopped fresh
    chervil, chives and tarragon
1 cup olive oil
pinch of ground coriander

Halve the radishes, or cut into quarters if large, and mix with the chopped parsley. Season with pepper, if used. Cook the asparagus, carrots and turnips separately in batches of the stock until *al dente*; just tender but still slightly crisp. Drain the vegetables, reserving the stock. Measure 750 ml/1¼ pints/3 cups stock, adding

more liquid and stock (bouillon) cubes as necessary to give this volume of highly-flavoured stock. Strain through a double thickness of muslin (cheesecloth) and, if the stock is not absolutely clear, clarify with egg white (see page 94). Leave until lukewarm.

Dissolve the gelatine in a little of the stock then stir into the remainder and allow to cool. When the stock begins to thicken, rinse out a 1 kg/2 lb loaf tin or terrine with cold water and pour in jellied stock to a depth of 1 cm/½ inch. Leave in the refrigerator to set.

Add a layer of each vegetable and avocado in turn, covering with jellied stock and allowing to set between each addition. Finish with a layer of jellied stock. This terrine may be kept in the refrigerator for up to 2 days.

Prepare the sauce by mashing the avocado flesh to a purée and mixing with other ingredients. To serve, turn out of the terrine and cut into thick slices. Hand the sauce separately.
SERVES 8

FONDS D'ARTICHAUT MAÎTRE CORBEAU

Artichoke Hearts with Eggs

It is always gratifying when one's high opinion of a restaurant is confirmed and the pleasant little *auberge* in the hamlet of Ezy-sur-Eure, where we tasted this starter, was recently awarded a gastronomic star.

Metric/Imperial
4 large fresh artichokes or 4 large canned artichoke hearts
100 g/4 oz mushrooms, finely chopped
2 × 15 ml spoons/2 tablespoons vinegar
4 eggs
200 ml/⅓ pint double cream
1 egg yolk
salt
freshly ground black pepper

American
4 large fresh artichokes or 4 large canned artichoke hearts
1 cup finely chopped mushrooms
2 tablespoons vinegar
4 eggs
1 cup heavy cream
1 egg yolk
salt
freshly ground black pepper

If using fresh artichokes, snip off the tops of the leaves and cut off the stalks. Cook in boiling salted water for 25 to 30 minutes, or until the bases feel tender. Drain, pull off all the leaves and remove the choke. If using tinned artichoke hearts, heat thoroughly in a colander over boiling water.

Cook the mushrooms in a pan over low heat until moistened with their own juice. Add the vinegar to a shallow pan of simmering water and lightly poach the eggs for about 2 minutes. Meanwhile heat the cream in a pan and simmer until it has reduced by about half. Take off the heat, beat in the egg yolk and add salt and pepper to taste.

Place a few softened mushrooms on each artichoke heart, lay a poached egg on top and pour the sauce over. Serve hot.
SERVES 4

BARBUE AU CIDRE

Fish Cooked in Cider

Vatel, the chef of the Maître Corbeau in Ezy-sur-Eure, showed us this superb way to serve brill or turbot in a rich, creamy cider-flavoured sauce. Although not strictly *à la française*, you could cook cod or haddock in this manner.

Metric/Imperial
1 brill or turbot, weighing about 1.5 kg/ 3 lb
500 ml/18 fl oz dry cider
small glass of dry white wine
4 shallots, finely chopped
salt
freshly ground black pepper
200 ml/⅓ pint double cream

American
1 flounder or turbot, weighing about 3 lb
2¼ cups dry hard cider
small glass of dry white wine
4 shallots, finely chopped
salt
freshly ground black pepper
1 cup heavy cream

Fillet the fish and remove skin. Put bones and trimmings into a pan with the cider, wine, shallots, salt and pepper. Bring to boil and simmer until reduced by about half. Lay the fillets in a well buttered ovenproof dish. Season with salt and pepper and moisten with a little of the simmering stock. Bake in a preheated moderately hot oven (190°C/375°F/Gas Mark 5) for 10 to 15 minutes.

Strain the reduced stock through muslin (cheesecloth) into a pan. Stir in the cream and simmer, stirring, until reduced and thickened. Place the fish in a serving dish and coat with sauce.
SERVES 4

Terrine de Petits Légumes Frais

CASSOLETTE DE HOMARD À LA CRÈME D'ESTRAGON

Lobster with Cream and Tarragon

Metric/Imperial
1 live lobster, weighing about 1 kg/2 lb
25 g/1 oz butter
2 × 15 ml spoons/2 tablespoons oil
5 × 15 ml spoons/5 tablespoons Calvados
100 ml/7 tablespoons dry white wine
100 ml/7 tablespoons court-bouillon
   (see page 94)
bouquet garni
salt
freshly ground black pepper
400 ml/⅔ pint double cream
2 × 15 ml spoons/2 tablespoons chopped
   fresh tarragon
GARNISH:
fleurons (see opposite)

American
1 live lobster, weighing about 2 lb
2 tablespoons butter
2 tablespoons oil
5 tablespoons Calvados
7 tablespoons dry white wine
7 tablespoons court-bouillon (see page
   94)
bouquet garni
salt
freshly ground black pepper
1¾ cups heavy cream
2 tablespoons chopped fresh tarragon
GARNISH:
fleurons (see opposite)

Kill the lobster by giving it a sharp blow on the top of the head. Detach the claws. Split the lobster in half lengthwise through the head, tail and shell. Discard the grey sac in the head and black line running through the body. Cut the tail into sections.

Heat the butter and oil in a pan, add the lobster and fry over a brisk heat, shaking the pan, until the shell has turned red and the flesh has stiffened. Drain off the cooking fat and *déglacez* the pan with Calvados. Add the wine, court-bouillon, bouquet garni, salt and pepper. Cook very gently for 10 minutes.

Take out the lobster and, when cool enough to handle, remove the shell. Divide the lobster meat between 4 warmed serving bowls and keep hot.

Stir the cream into the cooking liquor and simmer, stirring, until reduced and thickened. Strain, add the tarragon and check seasoning. Pour sauce over the lobster. Serve hot, accompanied by *fleurons*.
SERVES 4

FLEURONS

Puff Pastry Crescents

Metric/Imperial
PÂTE FEUILLETÉE:
225 g/8 oz plain flour
1 × 5 ml spoon/1 teaspoon salt
225 g/8 oz butter
150 ml/¼ pint chilled water
½ teaspoon lemon juice

American
PÂTE FEUILLETÉE:
2 cups all-purpose flour
1 teaspoon salt
1 cup butter
⅔ cup chilled water
½ teaspoon lemon juice

Sift the flour and salt into a bowl. Cut 50 g/2 oz/¼ cup of the butter into pieces and rub into the flour, using fingertips. Add water and lemon juice and mix to a firm dough, using a round-bladed knife.

Roll dough to an 18 cm/7 inch square. Flatten remaining butter into a slab and place in centre of the dough. Fold the edges of the dough over to completely encase the butter. Roll out to a rectangle, about 30 × 18 cm/12 × 7 inches. Fold into three and press the edges together lightly to seal. Place in a polythene (plastic) bag and chill in the refrigerator for 20 minutes.

Roll out pastry, with the raw edges to one side. Fold and chill as before. Repeat rolling, folding and chilling 4 times.

To shape the *fleurons*; roll out the pastry thinly and cut into crescents or decorative shapes of choice. Bake in a preheated hot oven 230°C/450°F/Gas Mark 8) for 15 to 20 minutes until well risen and golden brown.
MAKES 8 TO 12

TRUITE PHILIBERT DELORME

Stuffed Trout with Banana

Philibert Delorme was a 16th Century architect of renown. He built the Tuileries in Paris but his masterpiece in this region is the splendid château at Anet. Here at the Hotel Au Grand Saint Martin, Jean Dartix has created this unusual trout dish in his honour.

Metric/Imperial
225 g/8 oz mushrooms, finely chopped
2 shallots, finely chopped
6 × 15 ml spoons/6 tablespoons oil
juice of ½ lemon
50 g/2 oz mousse de foie, pâté de foie
   gras or best pâté
1 egg yolk
2 × 15 ml spoons/2 tablespoons chopped
   mixed fresh herbs
150 g/5 oz butter, softened
salt
freshly ground black pepper
6 trout, cleaned, with heads on
200 ml/⅓ pint dry white wine
3 bananas, halved lengthwise
250 ml/8 fl oz double cream

American
2 cups finely chopped mushrooms
2 shallots, finely chopped
6 tablespoons oil
juice of ½ lemon
2 oz mousse de foie, pâté de foie gras or
   best pâté
1 egg yolk
2 tablespoons chopped mixed fresh
   herbs
½ cup + 2 tablespoons softened butter
salt
freshly ground black pepper
6 trout, cleaned, with heads on
1 cup dry white wine
3 bananas, halved lengthwise
1 cup heavy cream

Sauté the mushrooms and half the shallots in the oil over low heat until softened. Add the lemon juice and, when all moisture has evaporated, transfer to a bowl and allow to cool. Add the mousse or pâté, egg yolk, herbs, 50 g/2 oz butter, salt and pepper. Mash ingredients together to form a smooth stuffing.

Slit the trout along the backbone between head and tail, working the knife along each side of the bones. Snap the backbone at each end and slide out neatly. Stuff the trout and lay in a lightly buttered flameproof dish. Dot with 25 g/1 oz/ 2 tablespoons of remaining butter and add the rest of the shallot. Pour wine over trout and cook in a preheated moderately hot oven (200°C/400°F/Gas Mark 6) for 10 minutes, or until tender.

Meanwhile, melt the rest of the butter in a shallow pan and when it begins to colour, add the bananas and brown on both sides. Lay the trout carefully on a warmed serving dish and place a half banana along each; keep hot. Pour the cream into the trout cooking dish and simmer, stirring, until reduced to a thick, rich consistency. Pour over the fish and serve at once.
SERVES 6

Truite Philibert Delorme, Cassolette de Homard à la Crème d'Estragon with Fleurons

CANARD AUX PÊCHES

Duck with Peaches

Metric/Imperial

1 duckling, weighing about 1.5 kg/
    3–3½ lb
salt
freshly ground black pepper
2 carrots, finely chopped
1 onion, finely chopped
sprig of fresh thyme
1 bay leaf
juice of 1 lemon
300 ml/½ pint demi-glace or fond brun
    (see page 94)
8 small peaches, peeled, halved and
    stoned
25 g/1 oz butter

American

1 duckling, weighing about 3–3½ lb
salt
freshly ground black pepper
2 carrots, finely chopped
1 onion, finely chopped
sprig of fresh thyme
1 bay leaf
juice of 1 lemon
1¼ cups demi-glace or fond brun
    (see page 94)
8 small peaches, peeled, halved and
    pitted
2 tablespoons butter

Lightly season the duck with salt and pepper. Roast in a preheated moderately hot oven (200°C/400°F/Gas Mark 6) for 35 minutes or until tender but still pink. Turn the duck over halfway through cooking and baste with the pan juices occasionally. Cut the duck into serving pieces and keep warm.

Skim the fat off the pan juices and add the carrots, onion, herbs and lemon juice. Place over moderate heat. Stir in the *demi-glace* or *fond brun* and simmer until reduced by about half.

Meanwhile, poach the peaches in a little boiling water until just tender then brown lightly in the butter. Arrange the pieces of duck and the peaches on a serving dish. Strain the sauce finely and pour it over the duck. Serve immediately.
SERVES 4

CANETON À LA BIGARADE

Duck with Bitter Oranges

Metric/Imperial

3 ducklings, each weighing about 1.5 kg/
    3–3½ lb
ESPAGNOLE SAUCE:
50 g/2 oz butter
2 carrots, diced
2 onions, diced
100 g/4 oz streaky bacon, diced
50 g/2 oz plain flour
1 litre/1¾ pints brown stock
bouquet garni
4 × 15 ml spoons/4 tablespoons tomato
    purée
salt
freshly ground black pepper

2 lemons
8 small Seville or other bitter oranges
250 g/9 oz sugar (preferably lump)
250 ml/8 fl oz wine vinegar
250 ml/8 fl oz dry white wine
GARNISH:
few orange slices, halved

American

3 ducklings, each weighing about 3–3½ lb
ESPAGNOLE SAUCE:
¼ cup butter
2 carrots, diced
2 onions, diced
6 slices bacon, diced
½ cup all-purpose flour
4¼ cups brown stock
bouquet garni
4 tablespoons tomato paste
salt
freshly ground black pepper

2 lemons
8 small Seville or other bitter oranges
1 cup + 2 tablespoons sugar (preferably
    lump)
1 cup wine vinegar
1 cup dry white wine
GARNISH:
few orange slices, halved

Caneton à la Bigarade

Prick the ducks and roast in a preheated moderately hot oven (200°C/400°F/Gas Mark 6) for about 35 minutes, turning halfway through cooking. The ducks should be slightly underdone.

Meanwhile prepare the Espagnole sauce: melt the butter and fry the carrots, onions and bacon until lightly browned. Stir in flour and cook until the roux is brown. Blend in the stock. Add the bouquet garni, tomato purée (paste) and seasoning. Cover and simmer for 45 minutes then strain.

Cut the wings and legs from the ducks. Remove breast from bone and cut into long fillets. Keep the pieces of meat covered. Chop the carcasses and reserve. Thinly pare the zest from the lemons and four of the oranges, using a potato peeler. Cut the zest into thin strips and blanch in boiling water for 5 minutes. Drain and reserve. Chop all of the fruit.

Dissolve sugar in vinegar, stirring, over moderate heat. Bring to the boil and cook steadily until the syrup turns golden brown. Take off the heat and carefully add the chopped fruit. Return to moderate heat and cook for 5 minutes. Add the wine, Espagnole sauce and duck carcasses. Season to taste and simmer gently for 2 hours, skimming as necessary.

Strain the sauce finely into another pan. Add the duck pieces and simmer gently for about 5 minutes until heated through. Arrange duck on a warm serving dish and pour the sauce over. Top with the orange and lemon zest and garnish with fresh orange slices.

SERVES 10 TO 12

PIGEON AU POT

The addition of *foie gras* to this farmer's dish transforms it to *haute cuisine*. Ideally it should be raw, fresh but canned *bloc foie gras* may be used instead. M. Meneau cooked this dish for us in an earthenware pot on a fire-mat over low heat, but a large flameproof casserole will do.

Metric/Imperial
4 tender young pigeons, plucked
50 g/2 oz butter
225 g/8 oz small turnips
225 g/8 oz small carrots
225 g/8 oz leeks
1 litre/1¾ pints well-flavoured chicken stock
salt
freshly ground black pepper
200 g/7 oz foie gras

American
4 tender young pigeons, plucked
4 tablespoons butter
½ lb small turnips

Pigeon au Pot

½ lb small carrots
½ lb leeks
4¼ cups well-flavored chicken stock
salt
freshly ground black pepper
7 oz foie gras

Draw and truss the pigeons, reserving hearts and livers. Sauté the pigeons in the butter over low heat for 20 minutes or until evenly browned.

Meanwhile, cut the vegetables into even-sized pieces. Bring the stock to the boil, add the turnips and carrots and cook for 4 minutes. Put in the pigeons and leeks. Check the stock seasoning, adding salt and pepper if necessary. Simmer for 20 minutes before adding the hearts and livers. Cook for 4 minutes then finally add the *foie gras*. Simmer for 4 minutes, or less if using canned *foie gras*.

Transfer pigeons to warmed plates. Serve each pigeon accompanied by vegetables, liver, heart and a portion of the *foie gras*. Spoon over the cooking liquor.
SERVES 4

ROGNONS DE VEAU BERRICHONNE

Kidneys in Red Wine

Metric/Imperial

4 calves' kidneys or 12 lambs' kidneys
100 g/4 oz butter
salt
freshly ground black pepper
4 × 15 ml spoons/4 tablespoons Marc or
    Cognac
2 shallots, finely chopped
100 g/4 oz lean bacon, finely diced
12 button onions
12 button mushrooms
bouquet garni
1 clove garlic, crushed
300 ml/½ pint Sancerre Pinot Rouge or
    other red wine
2 × 15 ml spoons/2 tablespoons fond
    blanc (see page 94)
GARNISH:
chopped fresh parsley
fleurons (see page 44)

American

4 veal kidneys or 12 lamb kidneys
½ cup butter
salt
freshly ground black pepper
4 tablespoons Marc or Cognac
2 shallots, finely chopped
¼ lb lean bacon, finely diced
12 baby onions
12 button mushrooms
bouquet garni
1 clove garlic, crushed
1¼ cups Sancerre Pinot Rouge or other
    red wine
2 tablespoons fond blanc (see page 94)
GARNISH:
chopped fresh parsley
fleurons (see page 44)

Trim, core and remove fat from kidneys; cut into slices. Heat three-quarters of the butter in a pan and fry the kidneys over a brisk heat, turning them once only, for 3 to 4 minutes. Sprinkle with salt and pepper, pour in the Marc or Cognac and *flambez*. Transfer the kidneys to a serving dish. Add the shallots to the pan and sauté until golden. Sprinkle over the kidneys.

Sauté the bacon, onions and mushrooms in the fat remaining in the pan until lightly browned. Add salt, pepper, bouquet garni and garlic. Pour on the wine and *fond blanc* and simmer to reduce until thick and syrupy. Cut the remaining butter into pieces and stir into the sauce.

Add the sauce to the kidneys and serve sprinkled with chopped parsley and accompanied by *fleurons*.

SERVES 4

NOISETTES D'AGNEAU RENAISSANCE

Lamb Noisettes with Sauce

The local lamb, *agneau du Berry*, is noted for its quick-fattening quality. Due to pasture as well as breeding the meat is lightly interlarded with fat, making it incredibly tender but still lean to all intent and purpose. Naturally, the recipe holds good for any lamb.

Metric/Imperial

4 lamb noisettes (see recipe)
50 g/2 oz butter
3 × 15 ml spoons/3 tablespoons port
4 × 15 ml spoons/4 tablespoons dry
    white wine
1 × 15 ml spoon/1 tablespoon demi-glace
    (see page 94)
salt
freshly ground black pepper
GARNISH:
butter for shallow frying
2 slices bread, crusts removed
4 mushroom caps
2–3 mushrooms, finely chopped
1.5 × 15 ml spoons/1½ tablespoons
    mousse de foie or fine soft pâté

American

4 lamb noisettes (see recipe)
¼ cup butter
3 tablespoons port
4 tablespoons dry white wine
1 tablespoon demi-glace (see page 94)
salt
freshly ground black pepper
GARNISH:
butter for shallow frying
2 slices bread, crusts removed
4 mushroom caps
2–3 mushrooms, finely chopped
1½ tablespoons mousse de foie or fine
    soft pâté

Prepare the noisettes from best end of neck lamb cutlets (rib chops). Remove the bone and shape the cutlets into neat rounds; secure with string. Heat half the butter in a pan over brisk heat and seal the noisettes. Lower the heat and cook gently until the meat is tender but still pink inside. Take off the heat, remove string and keep hot.

Déglacez the pan with the port, wine and *demi-glace*, then simmer until the sauce has reduced and thickened. Whisk in remaining butter, a little at a time. Season to taste with salt and pepper.

To prepare the garnish, heat a little butter in a shallow pan and fry the bread until crisp and golden. Sauté the mushroom caps in the butter remaining in the pan until lightly coloured. Sweat the

chopped mushrooms in the fat remaining in the pan until soft. Mix the chopped mushrooms with the mousse or pâté and use to fill the mushroom caps.

Place the bread slices in a serving dish. Arrange two noisettes on each and pour the sauce over. Top with the stuffed mushrooms. Serve with sautéed spring carrots, baked pastry boats filled with cooked asparagus tips and *Fonds d'Artichauts au Purée de Petit Pois* (see page 49). *Petits pain* (French rolls) may be served as a further accompaniment.

SERVES 2

FONDS D'ARTICHAUT AU PURÉE DE PETIT POIS

Artichoke Hearts with Peas Purée

Metric/Imperial
2 fresh or canned artichoke hearts
100 g/4 oz shelled peas
salt
1 × 5 ml spoon/1 teaspoon flour
2 × 5 ml spoons/2 teaspoons butter
freshly ground black pepper

American
2 fresh or canned artichoke hearts
¾ cup shelled peas
salt
1 teaspoon flour
2 teaspoons butter
freshly ground black pepper

Prepare and cook the artichoke hearts as for *Fonds d'Artichaut Maître Corbeau* (page 43). Cook the peas in boiling salted water until soft. Drain and purée in an electric blender or pass through a sieve. Blend the flour with the butter to form a

Noisettes d'Agneau Renaissance with Fonds d'Artichaut au Purée de Petit Pois and other accompaniments; Rognons de Veau Berrichonne with Fleurons (page 44); Nougatines (page 53), Profiteroles au Chocolat (page 51)

beurre manié. Place the peas purée in a pan over low heat and whisk in the *beurre manié*, a little at a time. Simmer for 1 minute. Check seasoning and spread over the artichoke hearts. Serve as an accompaniment to meat or poultry dishes, or as a light starter.

SALADE PARISIENNE

Parisian-Style Salad

This salad is named after the *champignons de Paris* (button mushrooms) which are its chief ingredient.

Throughout France *champignons de Paris* are so designated to distinguish them from the dozens of other types of mushrooms in common culinary use.

Metric/Imperial

350 g/12 oz button mushrooms, thinly sliced
juice of 2 lemons
2–3 slices cooked ham
175 g/6 oz Gruyère or Emmenthal cheese, diced
1 lettuce
VINAIGRETTE:
2 × 5 ml spoons/2 teaspoons French mustard
salt
freshly ground black pepper
1 × 15 ml spoon/1 tablespoon wine vinegar
4 × 15 ml spoons/4 tablespoons oil

American

3 cups thinly sliced button mushrooms
juice of 2 lemons
2–3 slices processed ham
1 cup diced Gruyère or Emmenthal cheese
1 lettuce
VINAIGRETTE:
2 teaspoons French mustard
salt
freshly ground black pepper
1 tablespoon wine vinegar
4 tablespoons oil

Place the mushrooms in a bowl and sprinkle with the lemon juice to prevent discoloration. Cut the ham into strips, dice the cheese and roughly chop the lettuce. Prepare the vinaigrette by shaking the ingredients together in a screw-top jar.

Drain the mushrooms. Combine mushrooms, ham, cheese and lettuce in a salad bowl and pour the dressing over. Toss well.

Serve immediately, either as a side salad or, allowing more generous portions, as a light luncheon dish.
SERVES 4 TO 6

Salade Parisienne, Petits Pois à la Parisienne

PETITS POIS À LA PARISIENNE

Parisian-Style Peas

For this vegetable dish use fresh *petits pois*, if obtainable, or garden peas. Alternatively use frozen *petits pois* and reduce the cooking time accordingly.

Metric/Imperial
40 g/1½ oz butter
1 × 15 ml spoon/1 tablespoon flour
200 ml/7 fl oz water
4–5 shallots or large spring onions
0.75 kg/1½ lb shelled peas
salt
freshly ground black pepper
2–3 × 15 ml spoons/2–3 tablespoons
   chopped fresh chives
2–3 × 15 ml spoons/2–3 tablespoons
   chopped fresh parsley
3 egg yolks
few lettuce leaves to garnish

American
3 tablespoons butter
1 tablespoon flour
1 cup water
4–5 shallots or large scallions
4½ cups shelled peas
salt
freshly ground black pepper
2–3 tablespoons chopped fresh chives
2–3 tablespoons chopped fresh parsley
3 egg yolks
few lettuce leaves to garnish

Melt the butter in a large pan, stir in the flour and cook over low heat to make a roux. Pour in the water gradually, and stir until smooth. Add the onions and cook, covered, over a low heat for 10 minutes. Add the peas, salt, pepper and herbs and cook gently for another 15 minutes or until the peas are tender, turning carefully once during cooking.

Drain the vegetables and add the egg yolks to the cooking liquor, one at a time, beating briskly to ensure a smooth liaison. Stir the sauce gently back into the peas and serve immediately, garnished with lettuce.
SERVES 6

PROFITEROLES AU CHOCOLAT

Time and time again one finds a childhood favourite billed as a restaurant's *spécialité*, due presumably to a nostalgia shared by chef and clients alike. M. Quilleriet says there are no hidden secrets here; simply featherlight *pâte à choux*, perfect ice cream and 'the best chocolate in France', which he buys in Paris.

Metric/Imperial
ICE CREAM:
300 ml/½ pint milk
1 vanilla pod
1 egg
2 egg yolks
75 g/3 oz caster sugar
300 ml/½ pint double cream, lightly
   whipped

pâte à choux (see recipe)
CHOCOLATE SAUCE:
175 g/6 oz plain dark chocolate, broken
   into pieces
3 × 15 ml spoons/3 tablespoons water
40 g/1½ oz butter

American
ICE CREAM:
1¼ cups milk
1 vanilla bean
1 egg
2 egg yolks
⅓ cup sugar
1¼ cups heavy cream, lightly whipped

pâte à choux (see recipe)
CHOCOLATE SAUCE:
6 squares semi-sweet dark chocolate,
   broken into pieces
3 tablespoons water
3 tablespoons butter

To prepare the ice cream; heat the milk almost to boiling, take off the heat and add the vanilla pod (bean). Leave to infuse for 15 minutes before discarding the pod (bean). Beat the egg, yolks and sugar together until light and fluffy. Stir in the milk. Strain into a pan and cook very gently until the custard thickens. Allow to cool then fold in the cream. Pour into a suitable container and freeze until half-frozen. Stir thoroughly, then freeze until firm.

Make the *pâte à choux* according to the recipe given for *Éclairs au Jambon* (page 10). Spoon the mixture into a forcing bag fitted with a plain 1 cm/½ inch nozzle and pipe small buns, well apart, onto greased baking sheets. Bake in a preheated hot oven (220°C/425°F/Gas Mark 7) for 15 minutes then lower the temperature to moderately hot (190°C/375°F/Gas Mark 5) for 5 to 10 minutes until well-risen, puffed and crisp. Make a slit in the side of each profiterole and transfer to a wire rack to cool.

To make the chocolate sauce; melt the chocolate with the water in a bowl over a pan of hot water. Blend in the butter and beat thoroughly. Cool until the sauce thickens to a pouring consistency.

To serve; fill the hollow centres of the profiteroles with ice cream. Arrange about four profiteroles on each serving plate and pour the chocolate sauce over the top. Serve immediately.
SERVES 6 TO 8

NOUGATINES

Metric/Imperial
20 cm/8 inch sponge cake (see recipe)
PRALINE:
225 g/8 oz sugar
6 × 15 ml spoons/6 tablespoons water
225 g/8 oz unblanched almonds,
*   chopped*

butter cream (see recipe)
toasted slivered almonds for coating

American
8 inch sponge cake (see recipe)
PRALINE:
1 cup sugar
6 tablespoons water
2 cups chopped unblanched almonds

butter cream (see recipe)
toasted slivered almonds for coating

Prepare the sponge according to the recipe given for *Le Chantecler* (page 18) but turn the mixture into a 20 cm/8 inch round cake tin and bake for 25 to 35 minutes until well-risen and golden brown. Cool on a wire rack then cut into wedges. Trim the corners to give a smooth outer edge.

For the praline: dissolve the sugar in the water, stirring over low heat. Boil steadily until the syrup turns golden brown. Add the almonds. Cool slightly then spread over the flat sides of the sponge wedges. Pour the remaining praline onto an oiled board, cool then crush to a fine powder.

Prepare the butter cream according to the recipe given for *Le Chantecler* (page 18), using half quantities. Beat in the powdered praline. Cover the exposed sponge with butter cream and roll in the slivered almonds.

MAKES ABOUT 8 NOUGATINES

DÉLICE DE L'AUBERGE

Metric/Imperial
600 ml/1 pint ice cream (see recipe)
CRÈME CHANTILLY:
200 ml/⅓ pint double cream
40 g/1½ oz icing sugar

50 g/2 oz slivered almonds, toasted
150 ml/¼ pint Grand Marnier
SPUN SUGAR:
225 g/8 oz sugar (preferably lump)
150 ml/¼ pint water
pinch of cream of tartar

Tuiles aux Amandes, Délice de l'Auberge, Canard aux Pêches (page 46), Barbue au Cidre (page 43), Fonds d'Artichaut Maître Corbeau (page 43)

American
2½ cups ice cream (see recipe)
CRÈME CHANTILLY:
1 cup heavy cream
⅓ cup confectioners' sugar

½ cup slivered almonds, toasted
⅔ cup Grand Marnier
SPUN SUGAR:
1 cup sugar (preferably lump)
⅔ cup water
pinch of cream of tartar

Prepare the ice cream according to the recipe given for *Profiteroles au Chocolat* (page 51), adding 1 tablespoon coffee essence or cold strong black coffee to the custard before folding in the cream.

For the *crème Chantilly*; whip the cream and icing (confectioners') sugar until light and fluffy. Place a 3 cm/1¼ inch layer of ice cream in a 1.2 litre/2 pint freezerproof container. Cover with a 1 cm/½ inch layer of *crème Chantilly*. Sprinkle with some of the almonds and liqueur. Continue layering in this way finishing with the last of the almonds. Freeze the *délice* for at least 6 hours.

For the spun sugar; stir the sugar with the water over low heat until quite dissolved, then boil steadily until the syrup reaches 155°C/312°F and turns a light golden brown colour. Remove from heat, stir in the cream of tartar and leave to cool.

To serve, place portions of the *délice* in tall glasses or sundae dishes. Melt the caramel over a low heat. Using an oiled

Cobbled village street in Perche

wooden spoon, pick up strands of the caramel and twirl over the ice from a height to form threads. The spun sugar should harden enough as it falls to build into a sugar web over the dessert. Serve with *Tuiles aux Amandes* (see below).
SERVES 4 TO 5

TUILES AUX AMANDES

Almond Biscuits

Metric/Imperial
100 g/4 oz butter, softened
225 g/8 oz caster sugar
100 g/4 oz plain flour
4 egg whites
75 g/3 oz slivered almonds

American
½ cup softened butter
1 cup sugar
1 cup all-purpose flour
4 egg whites
¾ cup slivered almonds

Beat together the butter, sugar, flour and egg whites until perfectly smooth. Spread large spoonfuls of the mixture onto well greased baking sheets to form oval shapes, about 18 cm/7 inches long. Sprinkle with almonds. Bake in a preheated moderately hot oven (190°C/375°F/Gas Mark 5) for 5 minutes or until golden brown.

Lift off with the aid of a palette knife and drape each *tuile* over a rolling pin to cool. Repeat until all the biscuit mixture has been used.
MAKES ABOUT 16

Bourgogne, Bresse, Lyonnais

From its position and character this area might be termed the 'educated stomach' of France: a gourmet's paradise since Gallo-Roman times. With more great restaurants per hectare than almost anywhere, it's the birthplace of many *haute-cuisine* classics – rich, elaborate dishes lapped with cream and wine, opulent with truffles. Appropriately the *nouvelle cuisine*, which relies more on superb ingredients brilliantly cooked than on lavish extras, was born in the heart of all this extravagance. The late Fernand Point, archpriest of one of France's greatest restaurants, was first to preach the lighter touch – a philosophy further developed in Michel Guérard's *cuisine minceur*. Some of this gastronomic pride may stem from history. In AD 843, Charlemagne's empire was divided among his three grandsons: Charles the Bald received this area and founded the all-powerful Duchy of Burgundy, mightier than the Kingdom of France itself until it joined the Crown in 1477.

Fewer trimmings are not going to make for miserable meals! A veritable giant's farmyard and market garden in one, all good things of the table are here. Charrolais beef are reared as well as the famous blue-footed Bresse chicken, turkeys, guinea fowl and quail. Dozens of rivers, rushing to join the Saône and Rhône, teem with fish. So do the lakes of La Dombes and Bresse, which are also home for masses of water fowl – to the delight of sportsmen, diners and ornithologists. Fish are cooked in their own right or as *pochouse*, the local fish stew. The north is waist-high in soft fruits, especially raspberries, redcurrants and blackcurrants – hence the ambrosial Crème de Cassis liqueur. Many Rhône ex-vineyards have been replanted as orchards, yielding delicious peaches, apricots, cherries, apples and pears. There are butter, eggs, cream and cheeses a-plenty – our favourite cheese is Bleu de Bresse. For seasoning, add a spoonful of the 10,000 tonnes of mustard made annually around Dijon!

There's wine to please every palate and pocket, and it's fun looking for it! 'Dégustation gratuite' means the tasting is free at the *caveaux* (wine-cellars) though if you don't buy a bottle, it's only reasonable to leave a small grateful donation. The Romans brought vines to Burgundy, the Greeks did so even earlier along the Rhône. All manner of monks were responsible for great oenological advances, and the Revolutionary break-up of the monasteries' vineyards was a viticultural tragedy second only to the phylloxera disaster. As well as the wine *châteaux*, see the magnificent Hospices at Beaune, their charitable works supported by their wine. The Abbey at Cluny was another victim of Revolution, but its impressive remains can be enjoyed in this agreeable town – alongside the National Stud, built largely with stones from the Abbey ruins. Bressane villages can be attractive: there's an outstanding example at Pérouges, named after its pre-Roman Italian founders. From Lyon and historic Vienne, the Rhône passes renowned vineyards yet again. The old Tournon suspension bridge, used as a model for New York's Brooklyn Bridge, has gone but the views from the *corniches* from here on are unforgettable. A supreme drive in this district is in the south-west: the Ardèche river flows from Auvergne through memorable scenery and some really spectacular gorges.

GÂTEAU DE FOIE BLOND DE VOLAILLE DE BRESSE

Chicken Liver Starter

Foie blond is the Bresse chicken equivalent of *foie gras*; chicken, like the geese, are overfed so their livers become large, fat and *blond* (pale). Unlike ordinary livers, these are short-textured and can be mashed even when raw.

The 'roses' in the picture are made from raw potato, thinly sliced and dyed to match the tablecloth.

Metric/Imperial
SAUCE:
1 × 15 ml spoon/1 tablespoon olive oil
1 onion, chopped
1 shallot, chopped
100 g/4 oz carrots, finely chopped
100 g/4 oz celery, finely chopped
1.5 kg/3–3½ lb tomatoes, chopped
2 cloves garlic, crushed
1 bay leaf
pinch of dried rosemary
pinch of dried thyme
salt
freshly ground black pepper

8 foies blonds, or 0.75 kg/1½ lb ordinary chicken liver plus a little butter
1 clove garlic, crushed
pinch of grated nutmeg
450 ml/¾ pint single cream
8 eggs
GARNISH:
6–8 button mushroom caps
thin strips of truffle (optional)

American
SAUCE:
1 tablespoon olive oil
1 onion, chopped
1 shallot, chopped
1 cup finely chopped carrots
1 cup finely chopped celery
3–3½ lb tomatoes, chopped
2 cloves garlic, crushed
1 bay leaf
pinch of dried rosemary
pinch of dried thyme
salt
freshly ground black pepper

8 foies blonds, or 1½ lb ordinary chicken liver plus a little butter
1 clove garlic, crushed
pinch of grated nutmeg
2 cups light cream
8 eggs
GARNISH:
6–8 button mushroom caps
thin strips of truffle (optional)

Gateau de Foie Blond de Volaille de Bresse

To prepare the sauce; heat the oil in a large pan, add the vegetables and herbs and cook over moderate heat, stirring occasionally, until softened. Season with salt and pepper. Add enough water almost to cover the vegetables and simmer, uncovered for 30 minutes; sieve. The sauce should be of a thick pouring consistency; if too thin, return to the heat and simmer gently until thickened.

Rinse the livers and pat dry. If using ordinary ones, toss in a little hot butter for 1 to 2 minutes until stiffened. Mash the livers with the garlic, salt, pepper and nutmeg; sieve. Beat cream and eggs together and fold into the liver mixture.

Turn into buttered individual ramekin dishes. Place these in a roasting tin containing about 2.5 cm/1 inch of boiling water. Cook in a preheated cool oven 150°C/300°F/Gas Mark 2) for 25 minutes.

Carefully unmould onto a flameproof serving dish and pour the sauce over. Flash under a preheated grill (broiler) to brown the tops. To prepare the garnish; make a series of curved cuts, around the mushroom caps. Poach lightly in a little water. Place on top of the moulds and arrange the strips of truffle, if used, on top. Serve hot.
SERVES 6 TO 8

OEUFS EN MEURETTE

Eggs in Red Wine Sauce

Metric/Imperial
1 onion, chopped
1 carrot, sliced
1 leek, thinly sliced (optional)
1 clove garlic, crushed
sprig of fresh or dried thyme
1–2 bay leaves
450 ml/¾ pint red Burgundy or other red wine
salt
freshly ground black pepper
25 g/1 oz flour
50 g/2 oz butter
1 × 15 ml spoon/1 tablespoon vinegar
6 eggs

American
1 onion, chopped
1 carrot, sliced
1 leek, thinly sliced (optional)
1 clove garlic, crushed
sprig of fresh or dried thyme
1–2 bay leaves
2 cups red Burgundy or other red wine
salt
freshly ground black pepper
¼ cup flour
¼ cup butter
1 tablespoon vinegar
6 eggs

Put the vegetables and herbs in a saucepan with the wine. Add salt and pepper to taste. Bring to the boil, cover and simmer for 30 minutes. Discard the thyme and bay leaves. Pass the vegetables through a coarse sieve (strainer) and return to the pan with the liquor.

Blend the flour with the butter. Whisk this *beurre manié*, a little at a time, into the sauce over a low heat. Cook gently until the sauce is thick and smooth.

Add the vinegar to a shallow pan of gently simmering salted water and lightly poach the eggs for about 2 minutes; drain.

Serve the eggs coated with the sauce.

SERVES 6

JAMBON PERSILLÉ

Ham in Parsley Jelly

One of the prettiest items in the local *charcuteries* is *jambon persillé*, delicate pink chunks of ham in wine jelly, tinged a fresh looking green with parsley.

Metric/Imperial

1 mild ham, weighing about 4 kg/9 lb
large piece of ham or bacon rind
4 calves' feet
STOCK:
1 bottle white Burgundy or other white wine
4 large carrots, sliced lengthwise
4 onions, each studded with 2 cloves
2 sticks celery
6 coriander seeds
sprig of fresh rosemary
2 fresh sage leaves
12 black peppercorns
pinch of curry powder
1 bouquet garni
4 litres/7 pints water
PERSILLADE:
4 shallots, finely chopped
2 cloves garlic, crushed
75 g/3 oz butter
handful of chopped fresh parsley
2 × 15 ml spoons/2 tablespoons chopped fresh chervil
2 × 15 ml spoons/2 tablespoons chopped fresh tarragon

6 × 15 ml spoons/6 tablespoons Cognac
150 ml/¼ pint port
gelatine (as necessary)

American

1 mild-cured smoked uncooked ham, weighing about 9 lb
large piece of smoked ham or bacon rind
4 veal feet
STOCK:
1 bottle white Burgundy or other white wine
4 large carrots, sliced lengthwise
4 onions, each studded with 2 cloves
2 stalks celery
6 coriander seeds
sprig of fresh rosemary
2 fresh sage leaves
12 black peppercorns
pinch of curry powder
1 bouquet garni
8½ pints water
PERSILLADE:
4 shallots, finely chopped
2 cloves garlic, crushed
⅓ cup butter
handful of chopped fresh parsley
2 tablespoons chopped fresh chervil
2 tablespoons chopped fresh tarragon

6 tablespoons Cognac
⅔ cup port
unflavored gelatin (as necessary)

Soak the ham for up to 24 hours in 2 or 3 changes of cold water. Place in a large pan with the ham or bacon rind, calves' (veal) feet, cover with water and bring slowly to the boil.

Drain, add the stock ingredients to the pan and bring to the boil. Simmer gently, allowing 30 minutes per kg/15 minutes per lb, until the bone can be pulled from the ham. Take out the ham, strain the stock and set both aside to cool.

For the *persillade*; gently sauté the shallots and garlic in the butter until soft, then add the remaining *persillade* ingredients.

Skim the fat off the ham stock and reserve. Warm the Cognac in a small pan, *flambez* and stir into the cooled stock, with the port. Test the jellied stock by putting 3 spoonfuls on a saucer in the refrigerator. If the consistency of the jelly is not thick enough, add 2 or 3 × 5 ml spoons/2 or 3 teaspoons gelatine, dissolved in a little water.

Grease 1 or 2 large terrines or loaf tins, depending on size, with ham fat. Cut the cooled ham into chunks, about 2.5 cm/1 inch. Place alternate layers of ham and *persillade* in the terrines, finishing with a layer of ham; press down firmly. When the jelly is on the point of setting, pour over the ham, a little at a time to allow it to trickle through and fill the air spaces.

Leave in the refrigerator for at least 2 hours to set; it may be kept thus for several days. Serve straight from the dishes or turn out. Cut into slices and serve with mayonnaise (see page 58).

SERVES 25

Jambon Persillé

JAMBON PERSILLÉ PLUS VITE

Quick Ham in Parsley Jelly

The recipe above is obviously too much trouble for the average housewife unless she has a large buffet party coming up. The following is an adaptation easy enough for more 'everyday' use.

Metric/Imperial
1 kg/2 lb piece cooked ham
250 ml/8 fl oz jellied chicken or veal stock (see page 94)
250 ml/8 fl oz dry white wine
1 clove garlic, crushed
pinch of dried rosemary
pinch of dried sage
freshly ground black pepper
3 × 15 ml spoons/3 tablespoons brandy
1 × 15 ml spoon/1 tablespoon gelatine
4 × 15 ml spoons/4 tablespoons chopped fresh parsley
1 × 5 ml spoon/1 teaspoon dried tarragon

American
2 lb piece processed ham
1 cup jellied chicken or veal stock (see page 94)
1 cup dry white wine
1 clove garlic, crushed
pinch of dried rosemary
pinch of dried sage
freshly ground black pepper
3 tablespoons brandy
1 tablespoon unflavored gelatin
4 tablespoons chopped fresh parsley
1 teaspoon dried tarragon

Cut the ham into chunks and put in a saucepan with the stock, wine, garlic, rosemary and sage. Season with pepper. Bring to the boil and simmer gently for a few minutes to warm the ham through. Add the brandy. Soften the gelatine in a little cold water then stir into the ham mixture. Leave to cool. When it starts to thicken, stir in the remaining herbs and pour into a 1 kg/2 lb terrine or loaf tin. Leave in the refrigerator to set.
SERVES 6

MAYONNAISE

Metric/Imperial
2 egg yolks
1 × 2.5 ml spoon/½ teaspoon French mustard
1 × 2.5 ml spoon/½ teaspoon sugar
1 × 2.5 ml spoon/½ teaspoon salt
pinch of white pepper
few drops of lemon juice
300 ml/½ pint olive oil
2–3 × 15 ml spoons/2–3 tablespoons white wine vinegar

American
2 egg yolks
½ teaspoon French mustard
½ teaspoon sugar
½ teaspoon salt
pinch of white pepper
few drops of lemon juice
1¼ cups olive oil
2–3 tablespoons white wine vinegar

Beat the egg yolks in a bowl. Add mustard, sugar, salt, pepper and lemon juice and whisk until thoroughly mixed and slightly thickened. Add the oil, a few drops at a time, whisking continuously. As the sauce thickens add the oil more quickly, in a thin stream. Finally, blend in the wine vinegar.

Classic mayonnaise should be thick, shiny and not too sharp.
MAKES APPROXIMATELY 300 ML/½ PINT/ 1¼ CUPS

MINUTE DE SAUMON AIGRELETTE

Grilled (Broiled) Salmon with Sour Sauce

Metric/Imperial
4 salmon steaks, each weighing about 100 g/4 oz
SAUCE:
150 ml/¼ pint mayonnaise (see opposite – ½ quantity)
juice of 1 lemon
1 × 15 ml spoon/1 tablespoon chopped fresh chives
1 × 15 ml spoon/1 tablespoon chopped fresh parsley

American
4 salmon steaks, each weighing about ¼ lb
SAUCE:
⅔ cup mayonnaise (see above – ½ quantity)
juice of 1 lemon
1 tablespoon chopped fresh chives
1 tablespoon chopped fresh parsley

Place the salmon steaks between sheets of greaseproof (waxed) paper and beat gently to flatten. Prepare the mayonnaise, thin it with the lemon juice and stir in the chives and parsley. The sauce should be of a thin, pouring consistency; if necessary add a few drops of cold water.

Cook the fish under a preheated hot grill (broiler) for about 1 minute on each side; just long enough for it to become pale and stiff.

Transfer the salmon to serving plates. Pour a little of the sauce over each portion.
SERVES 4

ÉMINCE DÉ SAUMON CRU MARINÉ AU CITRON VERT

Raw Salmon with Lime Juice

We've long known that a suitable marinade can make raw fish not only palatable but delicious; this is an ideal method for salmon.

The lime juice imparts a fresh tangy flavour to the dish. Limes are imported and are available all year round from quality supermarkets and greengrocers.

Metric/Imperial

350 g/12 oz salmon, cut into 8 very thin slices
juice of 3–4 limes or green lemons
olive oil (see recipe)
1 × 5 ml spoon/1 teaspoon each chopped fresh chives, tarragon, parsley
salt
freshly ground black pepper
SAUCE:
2 × 15 ml spoons/2 tablespoons French mustard
4 × 15 ml spoons/4 tablespoons cream
1 × 15 ml spoon/1 tablespoon lemon juice
lemon slices to garnish

American

¾ lb salmon, cut into 8 very thin slices
juice of 3–4 limes or green lemons
olive oil (see recipe)
1 teaspoon each chopped fresh chives, tarragon, parsley
salt
freshly ground black pepper
SAUCE:
2 tablespoons French mustard
4 tablespoons cream
1 tablespoon lemon juice
lemon slices to garnish

Minute de Saumon Aigrelette, Émincé de Saumon Cru Mariné au Citron Vert

Beat the fish slices as thin as possible between sheets of greaseproof (waxed) paper and place in a dish. Mix the lime or lemon juice with an equal volume of olive oil. Stir in the herbs and seasoning and pour over the salmon. Marinate for 3–4 minutes, then drain off excess marinade.

For the sauce; blend the mustard and cream together, add lemon juice and seasoning to taste. Arrange 2 slices of salmon on each plate and garnish with lemon slices. Hand the sauce separately.
SERVES 4

ÉCREVISSES À LA NAGE

Crayfish 'in the swim'

This must be one of the simplest ways of serving freshwater crayfish (écrevisses) and cheap too, if you're lucky enough to live where they are still found. If not, substitute Dublin Bay prawns (jumbo shrimp) or ordinary prawns (shrimp).

Metric/Imperial
30–35 (live) crayfish
1 carrot, finely grated
1 onion, grated
1 shallot, grated
300 ml/½ pint Seyssel or other dry white wine
1 litre/1¾ pints water
salt
freshly ground black pepper
pinch of cayenne pepper
GARNISH:
10–12 radishes, trimmed
sprigs of fresh parsley

American
30–35 (live) écrevisses
1 carrot, finely grated
1 onion, grated
1 shallot, grated
1¼ cups Seyssel or other dry white wine
4¼ cups water
salt
freshly ground black pepper
pinch of cayenne pepper
GARNISH:
10–12 radishes, trimmed
sprigs of fresh parsley

Clean the crayfish (écrevisses) by plunging into boiling water. Drain and gut them by inserting a small knife in the opening near the end of the tail and drawing out the black intestinal tract. Wash under running water. The crayfish (écrevisses) must be cooked immediately after they have been gutted otherwise their juices will run out through the small opening.

Place the vegetables in a large saucepan with the wine, water and seasonings. Bring to the boil and simmer for 5 minutes then increase the heat. Add the shellfish and boil rapidly, covered, for 5 minutes. Take off the heat, skim carefully and leave until the shellfish are cool enough to handle.

Shell most of the crayfish (écrevisses), and discard the heads, leaving a few whole for garnish. Boil the cooking liquor to reduce slightly. For the radish roses, make a few cuts through each radish from the base towards the stalk and leave in a bowl of iced water to open. Arrange the crayfish in a deep bowl and garnish with parsley sprigs, radish roses and the whole crayfish. Pour the cooking liquor over.

Serve warm accompanied by a bottle of Seyssel or the same wine used to prepare the dish. The wine should, of course, be well-chilled.
SERVES 4

Écrevisses à la Nage

TRUITE EN GELÉE, SAUCE VERTE

Trout in Jelly with Green Sauce

This appealing trout dish is ideal for a summer party as it is prepared well in advance.

Metric/Imperial
4–6 trout
1 litre/1¾ pints court-bouillon (see page 94)
1 litre/1¾ pints white wine
GARNISH:
few slices each of tomato, carrot, lemon
1 truffle, thinly sliced (optional)
few fresh tarragon leaves (optional)
JELLY:
4 egg whites, lightly whisked
3 × 15 ml spoons/3 tablespoons gelatine
SAUCE VERTE:
300 ml/½ pint mayonnaise (see page 58)
2 × 15 ml spoons/2 tablespoons chopped fresh parsley
2 × 5 ml spoons/2 teaspoons each chopped fresh chervil and tarragon

American
4–6 trout
4¼ cups court-bouillon (see page 94)
4¼ cups white wine
GARNISH:
few slices each of tomato, carrot, lemon
1 truffle, thinly sliced (optional)
few fresh tarragon leaves (optional)
JELLY:
4 egg whites, lightly whisked
3 tablespoons unflavored gelatin
SAUCE VERTE:
1¼ cups mayonnaise (see page 58)
2 tablespoons chopped fresh parsley
2 teaspoons each chopped fresh chervil and tarragon

Clean and gut the trout, remove the backbone and rinse thoroughly. Pour the court-bouillon into a large frying pan (skillet), add the wine and bring to simmering point. Poach the trout in the liquor, very gently, for about 10 minutes. Remove from heat.

When cold, transfer fish to a serving dish. Garnish with slices of tomato, carrot and lemon. Complete garnish with truffle and tarragon leaves, if used.

For the jelly; strain bouillon into a pan and clarify with egg whites (see page 94). Cool slightly. Dissolve the gelatine in a little of the clarified bouillon, then stir it into the remainder. When the bouillon starts to thicken, spoon it carefully over the garnished trout. Leave in the refrigerator to set.

For the sauce; prepare the mayonnaise and stir in the herbs. Pour into a dish and serve with the trout.

SERVES 4 TO 6

Truite en Gelée, Sauce Verte; Galette Perougienne (page 62)

VOLAILLE AU VINAIGRE

Chicken in Wine Vinegar Sauce

In Burgundy, *poulet de Bresse* are used in this variation of classic *Coq au Vin*, spiked with the sharpness of vinegar.

Metric/Imperial
4 chicken joints
salt
freshly ground black pepper
25 g/1 oz butter
1 × 15 ml spoon/1 tablespoon oil
1 onion, finely chopped
200 ml/⅓ pint dry white wine
200 ml/⅓ pint wine vinegar
200 ml/⅓ pint strong chicken stock
8 triangles of fried bread to garnish

American
4 chicken portions
salt
freshly ground black pepper
2 tablespoons butter
1 tablespoon oil
1 onion, finely chopped
1 cup dry white wine
1 cup wine vinegar
1 cup strong chicken stock
8 triangles of fried bread to garnish

Sprinkle the chicken with salt and pepper. Heat butter and oil in a flameproof casserole and sauté the onion until transparent. Add the chicken and brown all over. Pour in the wine, vinegar and stock. Cover and simmer until the chicken is tender; about 25 minutes.

Serve chicken with the cooking liquor poured over. Garnish with the bread triangles.

SERVES 4

Crêpes Vonnassiennes

CRÊPES VONNASSIENNES

Potato Pancakes

Metric/Imperial
500 g/1 lb 2 oz potatoes
2–3 × 5 ml spoons/2–3 tablespoons milk
65 g/2½ oz flour, sifted
3 eggs, separated
3 × 15 ml spoons/3 tablespoons double cream, whipped
butter for shallow frying

American
1 lb 2 oz potatoes
2–3 tablespoons milk
⅔ cup flour, sifted
3 eggs, separated
3 tablespoons heavy cream, whipped
butter for shallow frying

Cook the potatoes in boiling salted water for 20 minutes or until tender. Drain and mash with enough milk to make a thick purée. Work in the flour, then the egg yolks. Whisk the egg whites and fold in. Finally fold in the cream. The mixture should be the consistency of very thick pouring custard; if too thick add more milk, if too thin blend in a little extra flour.

Heat a little butter in a large frying pan (skillet) and drop in scant 15 ml spoonfuls/tablespoonfuls of the batter to form small rounds. Fry for 1½ to 2 minutes on each side.

Serve these *crêpes* as an accompaniment to meat or poultry or, sprinkled with sugar as a snack on their own.
SERVES 6 TO 8

GALETTE PEROUGIENNE

Baked Pancake

Galette, according to where you are, may mean anything from a savoury pancake to a crisp sweet biscuit. In this recipe it is a yeast dough, rolled paper thin then baked and caramelized.

Metric/Imperial
25 g/1 oz fresh yeast
4–6 × 15 ml spoons/4–6 tablespoons warm water
350 g/12 oz plain flour
1 × 5 ml spoon/1 teaspoon salt
grated rind of 1 lemon
25 g/1 oz caster sugar
2 eggs, beaten
200 g/7 oz butter, softened

Oeufs en Neige

OEUFS EN NEIGE

Snowball Eggs

Metric/Imperial
8 eggs, separated
350 g/12 oz caster sugar
1 vanilla pod
1 litre/1¾ pints milk
spun sugar (see recipe)

American
8 eggs, separated
1½ cups sugar
1 vanilla bean
4¼ cups milk
spun sugar (see recipe)

Whisk the egg whites until stiff. Lightly fold in 225 g/8 oz/1 cup of the sugar. Warm the milk slowly in a large, shallow pan, with the vanilla added, to simmering point. Add spoonfuls of meringue and poach for 4 to 5 minutes. Lift out meringues with a slotted spoon onto a clean cloth.

Whisk the egg yolks with the remaining sugar until pale. Whisk in the warm milk. Return to a very low heat and stir until the custard is thick enough to coat the back of a spoon. Cool, then pour into a serving bowl and float the 'snowballs' on top.

Prepare the spun sugar according to the recipe given for *Délice de l'Auberge* (page 53). Lift up fine threads of the syrup, using a fork, and loop over an oiled rolling pin. Repeat until all the syrup is used. Gather the spun sugar carefully with the fingertips and drape it over the dessert. Serve cold.
SERVES 6

Chef du Chais pipetting a sample of Burgundy wine from a cask. This is commonly termed 'thieving'.

TOPPING:
40 g/1½ oz sugar
75 g/3 oz butter, cut into pieces

American
1 cake compressed yeast
4–6 tablespoons warm water
3 cups all-purpose flour
1 teaspoon salt
grated rind of 1 lemon
2 tablespoons sugar
2 eggs, beaten
¾ cup+2 tablespoons softened butter
TOPPING:
3 tablespoons sugar
⅓ cup butter, cut into pieces

Blend the yeast with 3×15 ml spoons/3 tablespoons of the water. Sift flour and salt into a bowl, stir in the lemon rind and sugar. Make a well in the centre and add the yeast liquid, eggs and softened butter. Work the ingredients together, adding as much of the remaining water as necessary to give a smooth, pliable dough. Knead thoroughly, then leave, covered, in a warm place for 1 hour to rise.

Turn onto a lightly floured surface, knead lightly and roll out very thinly to a large circle, about 60 cm/24 inches in diameter. (If preferred, make 2 smaller ones.) Place on a greased baking sheet. Sprinkle with sugar and dot with butter. Bake in the centre of a preheated hot oven (230°C/450°F/Gas Mark 8) for 5 minutes. Move to the top oven shelf and bake for a further 3 minutes until the top is brown. Alternatively brown under a preheated grill (broiler). Serve hot.
SERVES 6 TO 8

Auvergne, Limousin, Rouergue

Here is country which shows its age – impressively. For 500 million years it has undergone primeval shiftings, foldings, eruptions and other upheavals. Its final form has been achieved only after the birth of the comparatively young Alps and Pyrenees, which squashed the south and east edges of the Massif Central into precipices, creasing the rest into gentler folds. In the gigantic limestone hills, broken by outcrops of granite and basalt almost as old as time, many of France's great rivers are born and have worn spectacular gorges to run in. You can enjoy their dizzying beauty from superb roads cut in their sides, or from boats.

Volcanic peaks soar rustily or sheeny black; some of the craters are water-filled creating unexpected lakes in the sky. The high grasslands support millions of animals, which in turn produce scores of truly great cheeses. In spring they are carpeted with flowers – acres of miniature daffodils and jonquils, and in summer they enjoy a ceiling of larksong. This ancient stage was a fitting background for that endearing early artist, Cro-Magnon man. His domain spread into Dordogne and you really should seek the moving experience of seeing his cave paintings.

The modern Auvergnat is proud and self-contained, but welcomes those discerning enough to appreciate his homeland. Here the ancient crafts are still going strong, elsewhere they are being revived, and there are probably more artisans to the populated hectare in Auvergne than anywhere in Europe. Most are independent, though some work in factories – in the cutlery centre around Thiers or carpet industry of Aubusson, for example. If you want to participate, craftsmen in the Rouergue run courses for visitors. On a gentler note, you can visit Vichy: its curative waters were famed before the Roman invasion but its present elegance is Napoleonic and Second-Empire. Natural or not, the scenery is compelling: the churches on top of the rock pinnacles in Le Puy; the bony *causses* of Aveyron, grazed by the ewes of Roquefort; the great iron viaduct at Garabit; the weird and mysterious rock formations of Montpellier-le-Vieux near Millau, the Paiolive in Ardèche; imposing fortresses towering from vantage points everywhere like castles in the air.

The food is hearty, emphasizing what the isolated smallholder could grow or store when harsh weather immobilized him; home-grown vegetables, home-killed pigs and hens, such small game as he could trap or shoot, eggs and milk when they could be spared, fish from the unpolluted rivers and fruit from the lower slopes. As in most upland regions, *salaisons* (smoked hams and sausage products) are plentiful and good. Verveine du Velay, made from verbena, is a famous Auvergnat liqueur. At these altitudes great wines are out of the question but, in some lowland areas, vineyards destroyed by phylloxera have been replanted and you will rarely go short of a palatable local product to drink with your dinner.

Truly the secret heart of France, the Auvergne repays long slow exploration, whether by car, on foot or on horseback.

TOURAIN À L'AIL

Garlic Soup

This soup appears in different guises in many parts of France. In Aquitaine it is called *Tourain d'Oie*, after the goose stock and fat featured in its preparation.

Tourain à l'Ail is one of several dishes we photographed in the grounds of the Château de Castel Novel (see page 69). Excavations in the foundations of this old Manor House have unearthed Roman coins, although the name of the Manor only dates back to 1289. It has been the home of many famous families including the Abussons and the Jouvenels. It is now a delightful hotel with two Michelin gastronomic stars to its credit.

Metric/Imperial

6 large cloves garlic, peeled and thinly sliced
50 g/2 oz goose or chicken fat
4 large tomatoes, skinned, seeded and roughly chopped
salt
freshly ground black pepper
1 litre/1¾ pints well-flavoured goose or chicken stock
4 eggs, separated
6 × 15 ml spoons/6 tablespoons wine vinegar
TO SERVE:
few thick slices of French bread, lightly toasted

American

6 large cloves garlic, peeled and thinly sliced
¼ cup goose or chicken fat
4 large tomatoes, skinned, seeded and roughly chopped
salt
freshly ground black pepper
4¼ cups well-flavored goose or chicken stock
4 eggs, separated
6 tablespoons wine vinegar
TO SERVE:
few thick slices of French bread, lightly toasted

Sauté the garlic in the fat in a pan over low heat for 5 minutes. Add the tomatoes, salt and pepper to taste, and continue to cook gently for about 20 minutes. Pour in the goose or chicken stock and add a little more salt and pepper, if necessary. Cover and simmer for about 15 to 20 minutes.

Beat the egg yolks with the vinegar in a warmed tureen. Gradually pour in the hot soup, stirring constantly. Beat the egg whites until frothy. Stir into the hot soup to form white strands – *tourains*. Check seasoning before serving with toasted bread.

SERVES 4 TO 5

PANNEQUETS AU ROQUEFORT

Roquefort Stuffed Pancakes

Of all the mountain cheeses made locally all over France, few are as well-known as Roquefort. A French shepherd discovered that far from spoiling, milk curds left in the caves of Mont Cambalou turned to delicious cheese.

Even to this day, every springtime, nearly a million ewes climb to the sparse summer pastures on the high *causses* to graze. To be legally Roquefort, the ewes' milk must be taken to the shepherd's cave to be matured.

Metric/Imperial

100 g/4 oz butter
100 g/4 oz plain flour
600 ml/1 pint milk
pinch of grated nutmeg
salt
freshly ground black pepper
350 g/12 oz Roquefort or other strong-flavoured cheese
3 × 15 ml spoons/3 tablespoons double cream (optional)
8 crêpes (see page 18)
2 × 15 ml spoons/2 tablespoons fresh breadcrumbs
1 × 15 ml spoon/1 tablespoon grated Parmesan cheese

American

½ cup butter
1 cup flour
2½ cups milk
pinch of grated nutmeg
salt
freshly ground black pepper
¾ lb Roquefort or other strong-flavored cheese
3 tablespoons heavy cream (optional)
8 crêpes (see page 18)
2 tablespoons fresh bread crumbs
1 tablespoon grated Parmesan cheese

Melt butter in a saucepan over low heat. Stir in the flour and cook for 1 minute. Take off the heat and gradually stir in the milk. Return to a low heat, add the nutmeg, salt and pepper, and cook, stirring, until the sauce is smooth and thick. Crumble in the Roquefort and stir until well blended. Add the cream, if used.

Spread some cheese sauce over the centre of each *crêpe*. Roll up and arrange in a lightly greased flameproof dish. Spoon the remaining sauce over the pancakes and sprinkle with breadcrumbs and Parmesan cheese. Flash under a preheated grill (broiler) until golden brown and bubbling. Serve immediately, accompanied by a crisp green salad.

MAKES 8

Monsieur Savy preparing Feuilletées au Roquefort in the kitchen of the Hotel Moderne, Rodez

FEUILLETÉES AU ROQUEFORT

Roquefort Puffs

In the land of Roquefort and, not far from those magic caves, is Rodez, ancient capital of Rouergue. Near the

impressive red sandstone cathedral is the Hotel Moderne, where M. Savy used to run cookery classes in his hotel for any interested *pensionnaires*. In one session we watched him prepare this local *spécialité* – ideal as an hors d'oeuvre or for a buffet party.

Metric/Imperial
pâte feuilletée (see recipe)
0.5 kg/1–1¼ lb Roquefort or other
   strong-flavoured cheese, crumbled
beaten egg to glaze

American
pâte feuilletée (see recipe)
1–1¼ lb Roquefort or other
   strong-flavored cheese, crumbled
beaten egg to glaze

Prepare the *pâte feuilletée* according to the recipe given for *fleurons* (page 44), using double quantities of ingredients; chill for 20 minutes.

Roll out the pastry thinly to a large oblong, about 3 mm/⅛ inch thick. Trim the edges and cut into 10 squares, approxi-

mately 10 × 10 cm/4 × 4 inches. Place a spoonful of cheese on each square. Dampen the edges with water and fold one half of the pastry over to enclose the filling. Press edges together to seal. Knock up the edges, using the back of a knife.

Place on greased baking sheets and brush with beaten egg. Bake in a pre-heated moderately hot oven (200°C/400°F/Gas Mark 6) for about 15 minutes until the pastry is puffed and golden brown.
MAKES 10

ASTET NAJACOIS

Stuffed Pork

Enfolded in a loop of the Aveyron river, a castle-crowned hill dominates the valley. The idyllic village of Najoic clings to the crest of the promontory behind – a truly spectacular setting.

Astet Najacois is traditionally served cold with lettuce and mayonnaise.

Metric/Imperial
1.25 kg/2½ lb piece of boned fore-loin or blade of pork
7 × 15 ml spoons/7 tablespoons chopped fresh parsley
2–3 × 15 ml spoons/2–3 tablespoons finely chopped garlic
salt
freshly ground black pepper
oil for basting

American
2½ lb piece of boned top loin of pork
7 tablespoons chopped fresh parsley
2–3 tablespoons finely chopped garlic
salt
freshly ground black pepper
oil for basting

Prepare the meat 1 day in advance. Mix the parsley and garlic and season liberally with salt and pepper. Spread this stuffing over the inside of the meat, roll up and tie securely with string. Wrap in foil and leave in the refrigerator for 24 hours to permit flavours to penetrate the meat.

Return meat to room temperature. Place in a roasting tin, score the rind and baste with oil. Roast in a preheated moderate oven (180°C/350°F/Gas Mark 4) for 1¾ to 2 hours. Serve hot or cold.
SERVES 6 TO 8

ROGNON RÔTI AU VIN ROUGE ET BLANCS DE POIREAUX

Roast Kidney with Wine and Leek Sauce

Metric/Imperial
4 calves' kidneys
8 shallots, finely chopped
2–3 leeks, white part only, finely chopped
75 g/3 oz butter
250 ml/8 fl oz red wine
salt
freshly ground black pepper
225 ml/8 fl oz veal or beef stock
225 g/8 oz calves' or lambs' liver
flour for coating

American
4 veal kidneys
8 shallots, finely chopped
2–3 leeks, white part only, finely chopped
⅓ cup butter
1 cup red wine
salt
freshly ground black pepper
1 cup veal or beef stock
½ lb veal or lambs' liver
flour for coating

Trim the kidneys, leaving an even thickness of fat surrounding them. Place in a roasting tin and cook in a preheated moderately hot oven (200°C/400°F/Gas Mark 6) for about 20 minutes, until tender. Remove all the fat and pierce each kidney with a needle in several places to release some of the juices.

Meanwhile gently sauté the shallots and leeks in half of the butter until soft but not coloured. Add the wine and seasoning; simmer over moderate heat until most of the liquid has evaporated. Add the stock and simmer until the sauce has reduced and thickened. Check the seasoning, adding salt and pepper to taste.

Trim the liver and cut into 5 mm/¼ inch slices. Dust lightly with seasoned flour. Heat remaining butter in a pan and fry the liver slices for about 5 minutes, turning once. Slice the kidneys and arrange in a hot serving dish. Place the liver on top and coat with the sauce. Serve with *Salade Castel Novel* (see opposite).
SERVES 4 TO 6

After Najacois with lettuce and mayonnaise (page 58). In the background of the picture is the local version of *fouace*; found in pâtisseries all over France

SALADE CASTEL NOVEL

Mixed Salad

Metric/Imperial
1–2 endive or crisp lettuces
French dressing (see recipe)
2 chicken breasts, diced
40 g/1½ oz butter
1½ × 15 ml spoons/1½ tablespoons wine vinegar
GARNISH:
50 g/2 oz shelled walnuts, roughly chopped
2–3 hard-boiled eggs, quartered
12 chestnuts, simmered in water until tender
100 g/4 oz cèpes or other mushrooms, sliced, soaked in a little lemon juice, then drained

American
1–2 heads of chicory or crisp lettuces
French dressing (see recipe)
2 chicken breasts, diced
3 tablespoons butter
1½ tablespoons wine vinegar
GARNISH:
½ cup roughly chopped walnuts
2–3 hard-cooked eggs, quartered
12 chestnuts, simmered in water until tender
1 cup sliced cèpes or other mushrooms, soaked in a little lemon juice, then drained

Salade Castel Novel, Tourain à l'Ail (page 66) Rognon Rôti au Vin Rouge et Blancs de Poireaux, Flognarde du Président (page 72)

Place the endive (chicory) or lettuce leaves in a large salad bowl. Prepare the French dressing according to recipe given for *Salade Périgordine* (page 29).

Sauté the chicken in the butter over low heat until tender; about 10 minutes. Pour off most of the fat from the pan and *déglacez* with the vinegar.

Add the dressing to the salad bowl and toss thoroughly. Stir in the hot chicken pieces. Serve immediately, accompanied by the garnish items in separate bowls.
SERVES 4

TROUFFADE AUVERGNATE

Potato Cake

Variations of this dish appear all over the Massif Central. Tomme, used in this recipe, is drained, pressed but unripened Cantal cheese. Any soft creamy cheese may be substituted. Alternatively use a hard cheese, such as Cheddar or Gruyère and grate coarsely rather than dice.

Metric/Imperial
50 g/2 oz piece streaky bacon, diced
225 g/8 oz potatoes, thinly sliced
100 g/4 oz tomme, diced, or other
   cheese (see above)
salt
freshly ground black pepper

American
¼ cup diced slab bacon
½ lb potatoes, thinly sliced
¼ lb tomme, diced, or other cheese
   (see above)
salt
freshly ground black pepper

Heat the bacon in a frying pan (skillet) over moderate heat until the fat runs. Add the potatoes and cook for 5 to 6 minutes, turning constantly. Stir in the cheese carefully, without breaking up the potatoes. Season with salt and pepper. Leave over gentle heat for 10 to 15 minutes, until the base is crisp and brown.

Invert onto a warmed plate. Serve as an accompaniment to meat or as a supper dish on its own.
SERVES 2 TO 3

Trouffade Auvergnate

SAUCISSES AUX LENTILLES DU PUY

Sausages with Lentils

This recipe comes from Moudeyres, a tiny village above the Rhone valley, and uses the small dark green lentils from nearby Le Puy. Almost any dried pulse, such as split peas, chick peas (garbanzos) or other lentils, may be used; but be sure to adapt cooking times accordingly.

Metric/Imperial
225 g/8 oz lentilles du Puy or other pulse
   (see above)
3–4 rashers smoked bacon, halved
6 large pork sausages
2 onions, each studded with 3 cloves
bouquet garni
salt
freshly ground black pepper

American
1 cup lentilles du Puy or other pulse
   (see above)
3–4 slices bacon, halved
6 large pork sausages
2 onions, each studded with 3 cloves
bouquet garni
salt
freshly ground black pepper

Soak the lentils in cold water overnight; drain. Place the bacon in a large pan over low heat and shake from time to time until the fat begins to run. Prick the sausages and add them to the pan; fry, turning occasionally, until evenly browned.

Add the lentils, onions, bouquet garni, salt and pepper. Pour in sufficient water to just cover the ingredients. Bring to the boil, lower the heat and cover the pan.

Simmer gently for 30 to 40 minutes or until lentils are tender and liquid has been absorbed. Remove bouquet garni. Serve hot.
SERVES 6

SALADE AUVERGNATE

Auvergne Salad

Lentilles du Puy also make a tasty and sustaining salad with *cervelas*, similar to the German cervelat sausage.

Metric/Imperial
0.5 kg/1 lb lentilles du Puy or other
   lentils or chick peas
1 large onion, quartered
bouquet garni
salt
freshly ground black pepper
350 g/12 oz cervelas or other smoked
   sausage
DRESSING:
1 × 15 ml spoon/1 tablespoon Dijon
   mustard
2 × 15 ml spoons/2 tablespoons wine
   vinegar
6 × 15 ml spoons/6 tablespoons walnut,
   olive or corn oil
GARNISH:
12 spring onions
chopped fresh parsley

American
2 cups lentilles du Puy or other lentils or
   garbanzos
1 large onion, quartered
bouquet garni
salt
freshly ground black pepper
¾ lb cervelas or other smoked sausage
DRESSING:
1 tablespoon Dijon mustard
2 tablespoons wine vinegar
6 tablespoons walnut, olive or corn oil
GARNISH:
12 scallions
chopped fresh parsley

Place the lentils in a large pan with the onion, bouquet garni and salt and pepper to taste. Cover with water and bring to the boil. Simmer, covered, for about 30 to 40 minutes or until the lentils are tender but whole. Drain and discard bouquet garni.

Meanwhile, peel and slice the *cervelas* or other sausage and place in a salad bowl. Combine the ingredients for the dressing and mix well. When cold, add the lentils to the sausage and pour the dressing over. Toss carefully.

Serve garnished with spring onions (scallions) and chopped parsley.
SERVES 6 TO 8

Saucisses aux Lentilles du Puy, Salade Auvergnate and Roquefort cheese

FLOGNARDE DU PRÉSIDENT

Fruit Pudding

Flognarde is a traditional Auvergne baked batter pudding with apples or pears. The Castel Novel prepare theirs individually, with pears; the late President Pompidou enjoyed his so much when he visited that the dish has since been named after him.

Metric/Imperial
200 g/7 oz plain flour
pinch of salt
3 eggs, lightly beaten
250 ml/8 fl oz warm milk
2 large pears, peeled, cored and sliced
sugar for sprinkling

American
1¾ cups all-purpose flour
pinch of salt
3 eggs, lightly beaten
1 cup warm milk
2 large pears, peeled, cored and sliced
sugar for sprinkling

Sift the flour and salt into a bowl. Make a well in the centre and add the eggs. Blend thoroughly. Pour in the milk slowly, stirring constantly, to yield a smooth batter.

Generously butter four 10 cm/4 inch soufflé dishes or other straight-sided ovenproof dishes. Pour in the batter and lay the sliced fruit on top. Cook in a preheated hot oven (220°C/425°F/Gas Mark 7) until well-risen and firm; about 15 minutes. Sprinkle with sugar and serve immediately.
SERVES 4

Clafoutis aux Cerises

CLAFOUTIS AUX CERISES

Baked Cherry Pudding

Metric/Imperial
0.75 kg/1½ lb black cherries, stoned
4 eggs
pinch of salt
100 g/4 oz sugar
50 g/2 oz plain flour
50 g/2 oz butter
250 ml/8 fl oz milk
sugar for sprinkling

American

1½ lb bing cherries, pitted
4 eggs
pinch of salt
½ cup sugar
½ cup all-purpose flour
¼ cup butter
1 cup milk
sugar for sprinkling

Thoroughly butter a wide shallow oven-proof dish and put in the cherries.

Beat the eggs lightly in a bowl. Whisk in the salt and sugar. Blend in the flour. When smooth, melt half of the butter and beat into the batter. Finally pour in the milk, stirring constantly.

Pour the batter over the cherries and dot with the remaining butter. Cook in a preheated moderately hot oven (200°C/400°F/Gas Mark 6) for 35 to 40 minutes, until the batter has set.

Sprinkle with sugar and serve hot or warm.
SERVES 6

SPÉCIALITÉ AUX NOIX

Walnut Speciality

Metric/Imperial

pâte sucrée (see recipe)
3 eggs
175 g/6 oz brown sugar
2 × 15 ml spoons/2 tablespoons coffee essence
50 g/2 oz unsalted butter, melted and cooled
75 g/3 oz plain flour
175 g/6 oz shelled walnuts, chopped
BUTTER ICING AND TOPPING
175 g/6 oz icing sugar, sifted
50 g/2 oz butter, softened
few drops of vanilla essence
175 g/6 oz chocolate
3 × 15 ml spoons/3 tablespoons milk

American

pâte sucrée (see recipe)
3 eggs
¾ cup brown sugar
2 tablespoons coffee extract
¼ cup sweet butter, melted and cooled
¾ cup all-purpose flour
1½ cups chopped walnuts
BUTTER ICING AND TOPPING:
1⅓ cups confectioners' sugar, sifted
¼ cup softened butter
few drops of vanilla extract
6 squares chocolate
3 tablespoons milk

Prepare *pâte sucrée* as for *Tarte Normande* (page 20) and chill. Roll out thinly and line a 33 × 23 cm/13 × 9 inch Swiss (jelly) roll tin. Prick the base and bake blind in a preheated moderately hot oven (190°C/375°F/Gas Mark 5) for 20 minutes.

Whisk eggs, sugar and coffee essence (extract) in a bowl over simmering water until thick. Remove from heat and whisk until cold. Pour the butter around the sides and sift flour over top of the mixture. Carefully fold in both, using a metal spoon. Finally fold in the walnuts. Pour into the pastry case and spread evenly. Bake in a preheated moderate oven (180°C/350°F/Gas Mark 4) and cook for 15 minutes. Leave to cool.

For the butter icing; blend the icing (confectioners') sugar with the softened butter and vanilla, adding a few drops of water, if necessary, to soften the icing. Spread a thin layer over the sponge.

To make the topping; melt chocolate with the milk in a bowl over a pan of hot water. Spread over the top of cake and leave in a cool place to set before cutting into squares. If liked, decorate with piped butter icing.

MAKES ABOUT 12

Spécialité aux Noix

Mademoiselle Ernestine Couriolle making dentelle du Puy lace in Mondeyres

Alsace, Franche-Comté, Savoie

'This is fairytale country' says a huge coloured cut-out of Puss-in-Boots beside the road. You are leaving the lush pastures of Lorraine to climb the fir-coated Vosges into Alsace. These woods are awash with nursery stories and legends – some gruesome, some hilarious, some plain historical fact. Many of the *ballons* (round-topped hills) are bare of trees and provide summer pasture for amiable black-and-white Vosgienne cows. Munster cheese is made up here and some of the part-time dairies are run as *fermes-auberges* where you can eat or stay – marvellous for walkers exploring the hundreds of miles of signposted footpaths. Magnificent views for the less energetic are provided by a military road along the crests.

The Vosges fulfil their geographical function well and the sun is often warmer, the sky bluer, over the great vineyards on their eastern slopes. The *Route des Vins* runs through the foothills like a necklace on which the pearls are the old wine villages. Tumbled red roofs, narrow streets between painted and timbered houses, flowers spilling from every window – the whole enclosed in thick walls with towered gateways: despite wars, a gratifying number of these delightful little towns remain. Below are flat farmlands and the fabled Rhine, now pleasure-bent, leaving the bustling commercial traffic to the great canal. Watching the shipping in its tremendous locks is a popular weekend pastime on both sides of the border. Surprisingly it's the little river Îll, meandering through these flatlands, which gave the province its name – Îllsass.

Alsatian wines are undoubtedly the best all round in these three areas though Franche-Comté has two masterpieces little known outside France: Vin du paille and Vin jaune – a cask-matured, yellow, nutty wine. Vin du paille is regarded as the jewel in the Jura's *vigneron's* crown; like Sauterne, it is made from over-ripe white grapes, carefully picked in November and kept on straw for 3 months before pressing and fermenting. Outstanding fruit brandies and eaux-de-vie are distilled throughout the region, some from unusual products such as holly and, in the Jura, gentian root – which is intriguing, and supposedly medicinal. Savoie's specialities in drink are Chambéry, a delicious local apéritif, and, of course, Chartreuse.

All three provinces make fine country cheeses, perhaps the most famous are in Franche-Comté, including Morbier with its mysterious dark 'waistline' stripe. *Cancoillotte*, a fragrant dish of fermented cheese with butter and garlic is popular in this area. Apart from *choucroute* and *kugelhopf*, Alsace is world-famous for onion tart and proud of its *foie gras*. There are dozens of different sausages everywhere, some with curious names: *gendarmes* in Alsace, *Jésus* in Franche-Comté. Jura's farm-smoked hams and beef are superb. Throughout the region streams and lakes abound with fish, especially trout and pike; and when in Savoie, try to get a taste of *omble chebalier*, Europe's noblest fish.

The mountains get higher as you go south and east – with Mont Blanc supreme. Skiing rules the winter scene but the rest of the year is a delight too, with high lake resorts, excellent camping facilities, wild flowers and breathtaking scenery making it an endlessly rewarding holiday area.

PÂTÉ DE FOIE DE VOLAILLE COLMARIEN

Chicken Liver Pâté, Colmar-Style

Metric/Imperial

1 kg/2 lb lean pork, diced
1 kg/2 lb lean veal, diced
2 onions, chopped
50 g/2 oz fresh parsley, chopped
1 × 5 ml spoon/1 teaspoon ground mixed spice
freshly ground black pepper
salt
250 ml/8 fl oz Sylvaner or other dry white wine
350 g/12 oz chicken livers
1–2 × 15 ml spoons/1–2 tablespoons Kirsch
1 × 15 ml spoon/1 tablespoon Cognac
PÂTE À PÂTÉ:
1 kg/2¼ lb plain flour
2 × 5 ml spoons/2 teaspoons salt
350 g/12 oz lard
300 ml/½ pint water
beaten egg to glaze

American

2 lb lean pork, diced
2 lb lean veal, diced
2 onions, chopped
1½ cups chopped fresh parsley
1 teaspoon ground mixed spice
freshly ground black pepper
salt
1 cup Sylvaner or other dry white wine
¾ lb chicken livers
1–2 tablespoons Kirsch
1 tablespoon Cognac
PÂTE À PÂTÉ:
9 cups all-purpose flour
2 teaspoons salt
1½ cups lard
1¼ cups water
beaten egg to glaze

Combine the pork, veal, onions, parsley, spice, pepper and 1 × 5 ml spoon/1 teaspoon salt in a bowl. Cover with wine. Sprinkle the chicken livers with salt and pepper and moisten with the Kirsch and Cognac. Leave both to marinate for 24 hours.

To make the pastry; sift the flour and salt into a bowl and make a well in the centre. Melt the lard in the water, bring to the boil and pour into the well. Quickly, beat to form a fairly soft dough. Cover and leave to rest in a cool place for about 30 minutes.

Drain off the marinade from the meat mixture and the chicken livers. Roll out two-thirds of the pastry thinly and use to line a 30 cm/12 inch long pâté mould or a 2 litre/3½ pint/4½ pint loaf tin, pressing well into the corners. Fill with the meat

mixture, arranging the chicken livers evenly throughout.

Roll out the remaining pastry to form a lid, lift over the filling and pinch the edges firmly together to seal. Decorate the top with shapes cut from the pastry trimmings. Brush with beaten egg and mark 2 or 3 slits in the pastry lid. Bake in a preheated hot oven (230°C/450°F/Gas Mark 8) for 20 minutes. Reduce the heat to (160°C/325°F/Gas Mark 3) and bake for a further 2 to 2½ hours.

Serve with clarified jellied veal stock (see page 94), gherkins (sweet dill pickles) and crusty bread.
SERVES 10 TO 12

TERRINE DE RIS DE VEAU AGNES SOREL

Sweetbread Pâté

An unusual pâté with a delicate flavour, created by René Florance whose Auberge du Père Floranc near Colmar is a 'must' on any gourmet's itinerary in Alsace.

Metric/Imperial

1 kg/2¼ lb calves' or lambs' sweetbreads
salt
2–3 carrots, chopped
2 onions, chopped
2 sticks celery, chopped
25 g/1 oz butter
2–3 sprigs of fresh parsley
1 bay leaf
1 sprig of fresh thyme
pinch of grated nutmeg
freshly ground black pepper
150 ml/¼ pint white wine
450 g/1 lb lean veal, minced
450 g/1 lb lean pork, minced
225 g/8 oz cooked tongue, diced
175 g/6 oz pâté de foie gras or best pâté
350 g/12 oz mushrooms, sliced
50 g/2 oz truffles, sliced (optional)
2 × 15 ml spoons/2 tablespoons brandy
slices of pork fat or streaky bacon for lining terrine

American

2¼ lb veal or lambs' sweetbreads
salt
2–3 carrots, chopped
2 onions, chopped
2 stalks celery, chopped
2 tablespoons butter
2–3 sprigs of fresh parsley
1 bay leaf
1 sprig of fresh thyme
pinch of grated nutmeg

Terrine de Ris de Veau Agnes Sorel, Pâté de Foie de Volaille Colmarien

freshly ground black pepper
⅔ cup white wine
2 cups ground lean veal
2 cups ground lean pork
½ lb cooked tongue, diced
6 oz pâté de foie gras or best pâté
3 cups sliced mushrooms
½ cup sliced truffles (optional)
2 tablespoons brandy
slices of fatback or bacon for lining terrine

PALETS PRINSKY

Cheese Fritters

Metric/Imperial
pâte à choux (see recipe)
50 g/2 oz Beaufort, Gruyère or other cheese, finely grated
FILLING:
50 g/2 oz butter
50 g/2 oz flour
350 ml/12 fl oz milk
175 g/6 oz cheese (as above), finely grated
1 × 2.5 ml spoon/½ teaspoon grated nutmeg
salt
freshly ground black pepper
COATING:
1–2 eggs, beaten
fresh white breadcrumbs
oil for deep frying

American
pâte à choux (see recipe)
½ cup finely grated Beaufort, Gruyère or other cheese
FILLING:
¼ cup butter
½ cup flour
1½ cups milk
1½ cups finely grated cheese (as above)
½ teaspoon grated nutmeg
salt
freshly ground black pepper
COATING:
1–2 eggs, beaten
fresh white bread crumbs
oil for deep frying

Make the *pâte à choux* according to the recipe given for *Éclairs au Jambon* (page 10); adding the grated cheese after beating in the eggs. Place the mixture in a piping bag fitted with a 2.5 cm/1 inch plain nozzle. Pipe 12 choux buns onto greased baking sheets, spacing well apart.

Bake in a preheated hot oven (220°C/425°F/Gas Mark 7) for 20 minutes. Reduce the heat to moderate (180°C/350°F/Gas Mark 4) and bake for a further 15 to 20 minutes until crisp throughout.

For the filling; melt butter, stir in flour and cook for 1 minute. Blend in the milk. Cook, stirring constantly, until the sauce is very thick and smooth. Stir in the grated cheese, nutmeg, salt and pepper to taste. Allow to cool.

Place the filling in a piping bag fitted with a 1 cm/½ inch plain nozzle. Push this gently into the centre of each choux bun and fill with the cheese mixture. Dip in beaten egg and toss in breadcrumbs to coat well. Heat the oil in a deep fryer to 190°C/375°F and fry the choux buns for 1 to 2 minutes until golden. Drain on kitchen paper. Serve immediately.
MAKES 12

Soak the sweetbreads in cold water for 2 hours; rinse thoroughly. Blanch in boiling salted water for 4 minutes. Sauté the carrots, onions and celery in the butter until softened. Add the herbs, nutmeg, salt and pepper and place the sweetbreads on top. Pour in the wine and braise for 20 to 30 minutes.

Drain the sweetbreads, trim and cut into pieces. Combine the veal, pork, tongue and pâté. Mix in the sweetbreads, mushrooms and truffles, if used; moisten this forcemeat with brandy.

Line a large rectangular terrine with the pork fat or bacon and fill with the forcemeat, pressing down well. Cover with more pork fat or bacon. Place the terrine in a roasting tin, half-filled with boiling water and cook in a preheated moderate oven (160°C/325°F/Gas Mark 3) for 1½ to 2 hours.
SERVES 10 TO 12

TRUITE AU RIESLING

Trout in White Wine

In mountainous country you find trout, in Alsace the king of wines is Riesling; small wonder, therefore, that the Alsatians put the two together in cooking.

Metric/Imperial
100 g/4 oz button mushrooms, sliced
50 g/2 oz butter
25 g/1 oz shallots, finely chopped
salt
freshly ground black pepper
5 trout, each weighing about 175 g/6 oz
250 ml/8 fl oz Riesling or other dry white wine
200 ml/⅓ pint double cream
GARNISH:
5 lemon slices
paprika
finely chopped fresh parsley
fleurons (see page 44)

American
1 cup sliced button mushrooms
¼ cup butter
¼ cup chopped shallots
salt
freshly ground black pepper
5 trout, each weighing about 6 oz
1 cup Riesling or other dry white wine
1 cup heavy cream
GARNISH:
5 lemon slices
paprika
finely chopped fresh parsley
fleurons (see page 44)

Sauté the mushrooms in half of the butter, with a little water added, for 5 minutes. Place the shallots in a buttered ovenproof dish and season with salt and pepper.

Trim, clean and wash the trout, pat dry and place on the shallots. Season with salt and pepper. Bring the wine to the boil and pour over the fish. Cover with foil and bake immediately in a preheated moderately hot oven (200°C/400°F/Gas Mark 6) for 10 to 12 minutes.

Carefully skin the fish between head and tail, arrange on a warm serving dish and leave covered. Strain the cooking liquor into a pan and simmer uncovered, until reduced to a thick syrup. Stir in the cream and reduce further until the sauce is a fairly thick pouring consistency. Off the heat, beat in the remaining butter, a little at a time, to give the sauce gloss. Stir in the mushrooms.

Pour the sauce over the fish. Top each with a slice of lemon, half of which has been dipped in paprika and half in finely chopped parsley.

Garnish the dish with *fleurons*, cut into decorative fish shapes, and serve immediately with a crisp green salad. A bottle of Riesling, or the same wine used to prepare the dish, should ideally be served as an accompaniment.
SERVES 5

Truite au Riesling

FILETS DE SANDRE BONNE FEMME

Fillets of Fish in Rich Sauce

At the Domaine de L'Abbaye, Bernardville, salmon trout caught in nearby rivers are used for this dish. The fish has a delicate flavour and pale pink flesh. A delicious creamy sauce is the perfect complement.

Metric/Imperial

1 kg/2 lb filleted trout, preferably
   salmon trout
100 g/4 oz shallots, grated
450 g/1 lb mushrooms, roughly chopped
2 × 15 ml spoons/2 tablespoons chopped
   fresh parsley
salt
450 ml/¾ pint Riesling or other dry
   white wine
50 g/2 oz butter
50 g/2 oz flour
600 ml/1 pint fish stock (see page 94)
250 ml/8 fl oz double cream
4 egg yolks
freshly ground black pepper
GARNISH:
fleurons (see page 44)

American

2 lb fileted trout, preferably salmon
   trout
¼ lb grated shallots
4 cups roughly chopped mushrooms
2 tablespoons chopped fresh parsley
salt
2 cups Riesling or other dry white wine
¼ cup butter
½ cup flour
2½ cups fish stock (see page 94)
1 cup heavy cream
4 egg yolks
freshly ground black pepper
GARNISH:
fleurons (see page 44)

Wash and dry the fish fillets and place in a buttered ovenproof dish. Sprinkle with the shallots, mushrooms, parsley and a little salt. Pour the wine over and cook in a preheated moderately hot oven (190°C/375°F/Gas Mark 5) for 15 to 20 minutes.

Meanwhile, melt the butter in a saucepan and stir in the flour. Add the fish stock gradually, stirring, to yield a thick sauce. Transfer the fish to a serving dish and keep warm. Blend the cooking liquor and vegetables into the sauce; simmer for a few minutes to reduce.

Just before serving, beat the cream with the egg yolks and stir this liaison into the sauce. Check seasoning and spoon over the fish. Place under a preheated grill (broiler) to brown the top. Serve with *fleurons*.

SERVES 6

Filets de Sandre Bonne Femme

TARTE A L'OIGNON

Onion Tart

Almost every cook in Alsace produces a different version of onion tart; this one is very much a quiche with its savoury custard filling.

Metric/Imperial
PÂTE BRISÉE:
250 g/9 oz plain flour
1 × 2.5 ml spoon/½ teaspoon salt
125 g/4½ oz butter, cut into pieces
1 egg yolk
2 × 15 ml spoons/2 tablespoons water
   (approximately)
FILLING:
250 g/9 oz onions, chopped
50 g/2 oz butter
3 eggs
2 egg yolks
pinch of grated nutmeg
freshly ground black pepper
250 ml/8 fl oz milk
250 ml/8 fl oz double cream

American
PÂTE BRISEE:
2¼ cups all-purpose flour
½ teaspoon salt
½ cup + 1 tablespoon butter cut into
   pieces
1 egg yolk
2 tablespoons water (approximately)

FILLING:
2¼ cups chopped onions
¼ cup butter
3 eggs
2 egg yolks
pinch of grated nutmeg
freshly ground black pepper
1 cup milk
1 cup heavy cream

To prepare the *pâte brisée*; sift flour and salt into a bowl. Rub in the fat, using the fingertips. Beat the egg yolk with the water and stir into the flour, using a round-bladed knife. Add more water, as necessary to give a smooth dough. Knead lightly on a floured surface then chill for 30 minutes.

For the filling; cook onions gently in the butter until soft and golden. Beat remaining filling ingredients together in a bowl. Add the onions.

Roll out the pastry to 5 mm/¼ inch thickness and use to line a 23–25 cm/9–10 inch flan ring, standing on a baking sheet. Carefully pour filling into the flan case. Bake in a preheated moderately hot oven (200°C/400°F/Gas Mark 6) for 40 minutes or until golden brown and the filling is set.

Serve hot, or cold with a green salad if preferred.
SERVES 6 TO 8

COQ AU VIN JAUNE FLANQUÉ DE MORILLES

Chicken in Yellow Wine Sauce with Morels or Mushrooms

André Jeunet, of the Hotel de Paris in Arbois, not only has a Michelin gastronomic star, he has also been judged the best *sommelier* in France – and his wine-list reflects his passionate love for his native country. This recipe traditionally features the classic vin jaune d'Arbois or Château-Chalon, but any strong white wine may be used instead.

Metric/Imperial
4 chicken joints
salt
freshly ground black pepper
flour for coating
75 g/3 oz butter
200 ml/⅓ pint white wine
225 g/8 oz morels or flat mushrooms, sliced
450 ml/¾ pint double cream

American
4 chicken portions
salt
freshly ground black pepper
flour for coating
⅓ cup butter
1 cup white wine
2 cups morels or sliced flat mushrooms
2 cups heavy cream

Dust the chicken portions lightly with seasoned flour. Melt the butter in a large sauté-pan, add the chicken and cook gently, turning occasionally, for 20 minutes. Remove from the heat and *déglacez* with the wine. Add the morels or mushrooms and cream. Adjust the seasoning and cook over very low heat for 20 minutes or until the chicken and mushrooms are tender.

Serve accompanied by a crisp green salad, French beans or petits pois.

SERVES 4

CHOUCROUTE GARNIE À L'ALSACIENNE

Alsatian Sauerkraut

No chapter on Alsace could be complete without *choucroute*, which may almost be termed the 'Alsatian national dish'. The quantities – designed for the healthy Alsatian appetite – may seem rather large! If so, simply omit one or two of the suggested meats.

Metric/Imperial
1 gammon knuckle end, weighing about 1.25 kg/2½ lb
1 large onion, chopped
50 g/2 oz goose or pork fat
1.25 kg/2½ lb sauerkraut
freshly ground black pepper
5 juniper berries
1 clove garlic
2–3 cloves
200 ml/⅓ pint Riesling or other dry white wine
0.75 kg/1½ lb pork loin chops
350 g/12 oz piece smoked streaky bacon or salt pork
8 quenelles de foie (see page 81)
8 medium potatoes
6–8 Strasbourg sausages or frankfurters
225 g/8 oz pork sausages, grilled
salt

Kügelhopf (page 83), Tarte à l'Oignon (page 79), Choucroute Garnie à l'Alsacienne

American
1 ham shank end, weighing about 2½ lb
1 large onion, chopped
¼ cup goose or pork fat
2½ lb sauerkraut
freshly ground black pepper
5 juniper berries
1 clove garlic
2–3 cloves
1 cup Riesling or other dry white wine
1½ lb pork loin chops
¾ lb slab bacon or salt pork
8 quenelles de foie (see page 81)
8 medium potatoes
6–8 Strasbourg sausages or frankfurters
½ lb pork sausages, broiled
salt

(cheesecloth) bag. Check the sauerkraut for seasoning; drain and arrange in a mound on a large warmed serving dish. Cut all the meats into serving portions. Place the Strasbourg and pork sausages on the sauerkraut and surround with the meats, potatoes and dumplings.

SERVES 6 TO 8

QUENNELLES DE FOIE

Liver Dumplings

These are a traditional part of a *choucroute*, but are sustaining enough to make a course on their own accompanied by a green salad or other vegetable.

Metric/Imperial
450 g/1 lb pig's liver, sliced
100 g/4 oz lean pork, diced
1 onion, chopped
3 cloves garlic
1 leek, white part only
handful of fresh parsley
50 g/2 oz plain flour
salt
freshly ground black pepper
1–2 eggs, beaten

American
1 lb pig's liver, sliced
¼ lb lean pork, diced
1 onion, chopped
3 cloves garlic
1 leek, white part only
handful of fresh parsley
1¼ cups all-purpose flour
salt
freshly ground black pepper
1–2 eggs, beaten

Mince (grind) the liver, pork, onion, garlic, leek and parsley together. Work in the flour. Season generously with salt and pepper. Add enough beaten egg to bind the mixture and mix thoroughly. Divide into 4 equal pieces and shape into dumplings on a floured board.

Poach these, a few at a time, in a large pan of simmering salted water for about 15 minutes, or until they float to the surface. Lift out and drain. If preferred, the dumplings may be cooked in stock to impart more flavour. Serve hot.

MAKES 4

Coq au Vin Jaune Flanqué de Morilles

Soak gammon knuckle (shank end) in cold water for 2 to 3 hours. Cook in boiling water for 2 to 2½ hours until tender; drain.

Sauté the onion in the fat in a large flameproof casserole or heavy-based pan. Add the sauerkraut and pepper. Tie the juniper berries, garlic and cloves in muslin (cheesecloth) and add to the casserole. Pour in the wine and just enough water to cover the sauerkraut. Cover and cook gently for 1 hour.

Add the pork and bacon and continue simmering for 1 hour. Place the liver dumplings and potatoes on top of the sauerkraut and cook for a further 30 minutes. Meanwhile heat the Strasbourg sausages or frankfurters in a pan of very hot water for about 15 minutes.

To serve; lift out the potatoes, dumplings and meats. Discard the muslin

TARTE AUX CAILLES

Quail Pie

Metric/Imperial

PÂTE DEMI-FEUILLETÉE:
350 g/12 oz plain flour
1 × 2.5 ml spoon/½ teaspoon salt
175 g/6 oz butter
6 × 15 ml spoons/6 tablespoons iced water
1 × 5 ml spoon/1 teaspoon lemon juice

FILLING:
75 g/3 oz prunes, stoned and chopped
4 slices pineapple, chopped
3 dessert apples, chopped
2 bananas, chopped
50 g/2 oz raisins
pinch of ground cinnamon
2 × 15 ml spoons/2 tablespoons dark rum
100 g/4 oz belly pork, minced
175 g/6 oz pie veal, minced
25 g/1 oz shallots, chopped
pinch of grated nutmeg
freshly ground black pepper
225 g/8 oz foie gras or best pâté
8 hard-boiled eggs (preferably quails')
8 quail, plucked, drawn and boned
50 g/2 oz butter
3 × 15 ml spoons/3 tablespoons white rum
40 g/1½ oz blanched almonds, toasted
40 g/1½ oz walnuts, chopped
beaten egg to glaze
2 × 15 ml spoons/2 tablespoons port

American

PÂTE DEMI-FEUILLETÉE:
3 cups all-purpose flour
½ teaspoon salt
¾ cup butter
6 tablespoons iced water
1 teaspoon lemon juice

FILLING:
½ cup pitted and chopped prunes
4 slices pineapple, chopped
3 dessert apples, chopped
2 bananas, chopped
⅓ cup raisins
pinch of ground cinnamon
2 tablespoons dark rum
½ cup ground salt pork
¾ cup ground stewing veal
¼ cup chopped shallots
pinch of grated nutmeg
freshly ground black pepper
½ lb foie gras or best pâté
8 hard-cooked eggs (preferably quails')
8 quail, plucked, drawn and boned
¼ cup butter
3 tablespoons white rum
⅓ cup blanched almonds, toasted
⅓ cup chopped walnuts
beaten egg to glaze
2 tablespoons port

For the *pâte demi-feuilletée*; sift flour and salt into a bowl. Divide butter into 4 portions and rub one-quarter into the flour. Add water and lemon juice and mix to a soft dough. Chill for 30 minutes. Roll out on a lightly floured surface to a rectangle, about 45 × 18 cm/18 × 7 inches. Dot another portion of the butter, in small pieces, over the top two-thirds of the dough. Fold the unbuttered dough over the fat and the top third down. Press the edges together to seal. Cover and chill for 30 minutes. Repeat rolling, adding butter, folding and chilling twice more; turning the pastry each time so the raw edges are to one side. Chill for 30 minutes.

To make the filling; soak the fruit, together with the cinnamon and a pinch of salt, in dark rum for 30 minutes. Combine the pork, veal, shallots, nutmeg and seasoning to make a stuffing. Wrap foie gras around each egg. Press the stuffing and eggs into the quail and truss with cotton.

Heat butter in a large sauté pan and brown the stuffed quail all over. Warm the white rum, add to the pan and *flambez*. Remove cotton from the birds and allow to cool. Reserve the liquor.

Roll out two-thirds of the pastry to just under 2.5 cm/1 inch thickness and use to line a 30 cm/12 inch round pie dish. Cover with a thin layer of the fruit. Place the quail, breast uppermost, on top. Fill the spaces with the remaining fruit and the nuts. Roll out the remaining pastry, more thinly, to make a lid. Seal the edges and brush with beaten egg. Knock up the edges of the pastry and decorate the top with pastry leaves. Make a hole in the centre of the pie and glaze with remaining egg.

Tarte aux Cailles

Bake in a preheated moderately hot oven (200°C/400°F/Gas Mark 6) for 40 minutes. Reheat reserved cooking liquor with the port. Pour through hole in the pie. Leave for 10 minutes before serving.
SERVES 8 TO 10

KÜGELHOPF

Alsatian Yeast Cake

Almost as inseparable from Alsatian cooking as is *choucroute*, this yeast cake is often eaten as an accompaniment to coffee – sometimes for breakfast. Its distinctive moulds may be bought from good kitchen equipment shops or a large ring mould can be used instead.

Metric/Imperial
75 g/3 oz raisins
3 × 15 ml spoons/3 tablespoons Kirsch (optional)
25 g/1 oz fresh yeast
250 ml/8 fl oz warm milk
75 g/3 oz sugar
0.5 kg/1 lb 2 oz plain flour
1 × 2.5 ml spoon/½ teaspoon salt
2 eggs, beaten
200 g/7 oz butter, softened
50 g/2 oz almonds, chopped
icing sugar for dusting

American
½ cup raisins
3 tablespoons Kirsch (optional)
1 cake compressed yeast
1 cup warm milk
⅓ cup sugar
4½ cups all-purpose flour
½ teaspoon salt
2 eggs, beaten
¾ cup + 2 tablespoons softened butter
½ cup chopped almonds
confectioners' sugar for dusting

Soak the raisins in the Kirsch, if used, otherwise cover with tepid water and leave for 20 minutes; drain. Blend the yeast with half of the warm milk, 1 × 5 ml spoon/1 teaspoon sugar and just enough of the flour to give a thin cream consistency. Leave in a warm place for 20 minutes or until frothy.

Sift remaining flour and salt into a bowl; stir in the sugar. Beat in the eggs and the rest of the milk. Knead in the softened butter and continue to work the dough until it comes cleanly away from the sides of the bowl. Add the yeast mixture, beat for a few minutes, then cover with a damp cloth and leave in a warm place for 1 hour or until well risen.

Knead the dough on a lightly floured surface and incorporate the raisins. Scatter the almonds in a buttered kügelhopf mould or 30 cm/12 inch ring mould. Press in the dough; it should only half-fill the tin. Cover and leave in a warm place for 2 hours or until risen almost to the top of the tin.

Bake in a preheated moderate oven (160°C/325°F/Gas Mark 3) for 45 minutes; if the top appears to be browning too quickly during cooking, cover with foil. Leave in the mould for 30 minutes before turning out. Dust liberally with icing (confectioners') sugar when cool.

Serve with coffee or tea. Kügelhopf does not keep well and should preferably be eaten within 1 or 2 days.
SERVES 10

Sorbet Marc de Gewürztraminer (above left); Typical Savoie Market at the height of activity in the village of Oyonnax (below)

SORBET MARC DE GEWÜRTZ-TRAMINER

Gewürztraminer is a truly astonishing wine, fruity and spicy but with no cloying sweetness – there could hardly be a better accompaniment to cheese, especially Alsace's famous Munster.

Koefferkopf is an *eau de vie* distilled from the *marc* of Gewürztraminer (residue left after pressing the grapes). This recipe can be made with almost any fruit wine and corresponding spirit.

Metric/Imperial
100 g/4 oz seedless raisins
½ bottle Koefferkopf or other spirit
0.5 kg/1 lb 2 oz sugar
500 ml/18 fl oz water
½ bottle Gewürztraminer or other wine
juice of 2 large lemons
2–3 egg whites, according to size

American
⅔ cup seedless raisins
½ bottle Koefferkopf or other spirit
2¼ cups sugar
2¼ cups water
½ bottle Gewürztraminer or other wine
juice of 2 large lemons
2–3 egg whites, according to size

Soak the raisins in the spirit. Dissolve the sugar in the water over low heat then boil steadily, without stirring, for 5 minutes; do not allow to colour. Cool. Combine the syrup with the raisins, spirit, wine and lemon juice. Pour into a suitable container and freeze until partially frozen.

Whisk egg whites until stiff and fold into the sorbet. Freeze until firm. Serve with wafers or biscuits.
SERVES 6

Provence, Languedoc

To many, Provence means the *Côte d'Azur*, peopled with expensively bared bodies, but it has a truly breathtaking beauty: glittering sea, colourful cliffs and the pellucid light so beloved of painters. There are times when the beaches are empty enough to enjoy, and prices are not as high as you'd expect.

Inland Provence enchants: behind the coast are lemons, oranges and carnations and miles of lavender fields – have you tried lavender honey? Provincia was one of the Romans' earliest foreign settlements so there are awesome traces of Rome. The refreshing beauty of the Alpes Maritime, the scent of crushed herbs beneath your feet as you walk the scrubby *garrigues* and the picturesque villages are not to be missed. For historical scandal, visit the fabulous clifftop city of les Baux. Perched high above eternal olives, it was notorious through the Middle Ages for Courts of Love, wicked tyrants, peacock-crowned troubadours and wronged husbands serving lovers' hearts for their unfaithful wives to eat. Today, the village suffers no such unsavoury goings-on, and the eating is better too! There's a whole galaxy of gastronomic stars among local restaurants.

Fontaine de Vaucluse was much less lurid! Ever a poets' haven, Petrarch wrote his 'Lives' here while moping over unattainable Laura. Every spring an incredible torrent of water gushes spectacularly from a great hole in the hillside and the river Sorgue is born. Unbelievably delicate limestone specimens retrieved from this hole by Cousteau are in a tiny museum. A streamside mill makes paper in the 14th Century manner.

Prefer the natural scene? There's the Rhone delta, where the cruel *Mistral* loses its icy sting over the marshland of the Camargue. Here are the famous black bulls and white horses, the blaze of flamingoes in flight. Rice and salt are the unusual 'industries' in this region of birds and tranquillity, sand and water, wind-sibilant reeds, sunshine and enormous skies. Around this sanctuary are the civilized old cities of Avignon with half its celebrated *pont* still standing, Nîmes and Arles. Further north is another great spread of vineyards. Among the best known are Châteauneuf-du-Pape with enormous round pebbles between the vines, and Tavel with its chunks of chipped marble.

Strong-flavoured Provençal cooking once compensated for a paucity of raw materials: only goats thrived here so meat and butter were rare, hence the use of olive oil in cooking. Nowadays there are early vegetables, particularly small purply artichokes and asparagus, and fruit. Near Cavaillon where famous melons are grown, is a centre for the regional speciality of crystallized fruit. Fish stalls, heaped with unfamiliar gaudy species, rival flower markets in riotous colour. Provençal wines are extra delicious – seriously! – when drunk on the spot.

Sharing much Provençal character and food, Languedoc has an added dimension: new tourist growth. *Vin ordinaire* proving economically insufficient, vast mosquito-guarded swamps were cleared for vineyards. Resorts of beguiling architectural aspect now service the littoral in contrast to the ancient tiled ochre villages, still dreaming in the sun.

SOUPE DE POISSONS

Fish Soup

This is made locally with various Mediterranean rockfish. It is ideal for 'odd' fish varieties, particularly those which seem too small or too bony to eat.

Metric/Imperial
2 onions
4–5 cloves garlic
6 × 15 ml spoons/6 tablespoons olive oil
1 kg/2 lb small rockfish, cleaned
2 × 15 ml spoons/2 tablespoons tomato
    purée
2.5 litres/4½ pints water
bouquet garni
salt
freshly ground black pepper
2 potatoes, roughly chopped
pinch of powdered saffron
50 g/2 oz spaghetti, broken
ROUILLE:
2 cloves garlic, crushed
2 egg yolks
6–7 × 15 ml spoons/6–7 tablespoons
    olive oil
1 × 2.5 ml spoon/½ teaspoon powdered
    saffron
TO SERVE:
French bread, sliced and toasted
Gruyère or Cheddar cheese, grated

American
2 onions
4–5 cloves garlic
6 tablespoons olive oil
2 lb small rockfish, cleaned
2 tablespoons tomato paste
5½ pints water
bouquet garni
salt
freshly ground black pepper
2 potatoes, roughly chopped
pinch of powdered saffron
½ cup broken spaghetti
ROUILLE:
2 cloves garlic, crushed
2 egg yolks
6–7 tablespoons olive oil
½ teaspoon powdered saffron
TO SERVE:
French bread, sliced and toasted
Gruyère or Cheddar cheese, grated

Sauté the onions and garlic in the oil until soft and translucent. Add fish and tomato purée (paste); cook, stirring for 1 to 2 minutes. Pour in the water and bring to the boil. Add bouquet garni, salt, pepper and potatoes. Simmer for 30 minutes.

Strain soup into another pan, pressing as much fish through as possible. Add the saffron and check seasoning. Stir in the spaghetti and simmer for 10 minutes.

Soupe de Poissons

For the *rouille*; beat together the garlic and egg yolks. Whisk in the oil, drop by drop as for a mayonnaise. Add saffron and season with salt and pepper.

To serve; spread the toast generously with *rouille* and sprinkle with cheese. Ladle the soup into dishes and garnish with the toast.
SERVES 6

OMELETTE À L'HUILE D'OLIVES ET AUX TOMATES

Olive and Tomato Omelet

Good quality olive oil snould be used for this omelet to impart its characteristic flavour.

Metric/Imperial
3–4 × 15 ml spoons/3–4 tablespoons
    tomate concassée (see recipe)
2 eggs
salt
freshly ground black pepper
1 × 15 ml spoon/1 tablespoon olive oil
olive oil for shallow frying
2–3 black olives, stoned and sliced
chopped fresh parsley to garnish

American
3–4 tablespoons tomate concassée
    (see recipe)
2 eggs
salt
freshly ground black pepper
1 tablespoon olive oil
olive oil for shallow frying
2–3 ripe olives, pitted and sliced
chopped fresh parsley to garnish

Prepare the *tomato concassée* according to the recipe for *Petits Rougets du Bassin au Cerfeuil* (page 26). Set aside until quite cool.

Beat the eggs with the salt, pepper and oil, then stir in the *tomate concassée*. Heat a generous measure of oil in an omelet pan. When very hot, pour in the egg mixture and stir vigorously with a fork, shaking the pan over high heat, for about 30 seconds. As soon as the *omelette* begins to rise, slide onto an ovenproof serving dish.

Sprinkle with olives and cook in a very hot oven (240°C/475°F/Gas Mark 9) for 1 to 2 minutes until risen and puffy. Serve immediately, garnished with parsley.
SERVES 1

OEUFS TAPENADE

Anchovy and Olive Stuffed Eggs

This starter takes its name from the Provençal dialect – *Tapéno*, meaning capers.

Metric/Imperial
6 hard-boiled eggs
25 g/1 oz black olives, stoned
8 anchovy fillets
25 g/1 oz canned tuna fish
2–3 × 15 ml spoons/2–3 tablespoons
  capers
5–7 × 15 ml spoons/5–7 tablespoons
  olive oil
few drops of lemon juice
2 × 5 ml spoons/2 teaspoons Cognac
  (optional)
freshly ground black pepper
GARNISH:
few sprigs of fresh parsley
few olive slices

Oeufs Tapenade, Anchoïade (page 88),
Omelette à l'Huile d'Olives

American
6 hard-cooked eggs
1 cup pitted ripe olives
8 anchovy filets
¼ cup canned tuna
2–3 tablespoons capers
5–7 tablespoons olive oil
few drops of lemon juice
2 teaspoons Cognac (optional)
freshly ground black pepper
GARNISH:
few olive slices
few sprigs of fresh parsley

Halve the eggs lengthwise and scoop out
the yolks; reserve. Pound the olives,
anchovies, tuna and capers to a smooth
paste, using a pestle and mortar. Beat in
the olive oil, a little at a time, until the
mixture is a creamy, thick consistency.

Mash the egg yolks and blend into the
mixture. Add lemon juice, Cognac and
black pepper to taste.

Place in a piping bag, fitted with a fluted
nozzle, and pipe the stuffing into the hollow egg whites. Garnish with a few olive
slices and parsley. Serve on a bed of lettuce
as a starter or as part of an hors d'oeuvre
or buffet.
SERVES 6

ANCHOÏADE

Anchovy Dip

This *maigre* dish was traditionally used to keep you going while fasting before Christmas Midnight Mass. As a dip it makes an excellent entrée.

Metric/Imperial
2×50 g/2 oz cans anchovy fillets
3–4 cloves garlic, chopped
4×15 ml spoons/4 tablespoons olive oil
    (approximately)
freshly ground black pepper
chopped fresh parsley to garnish
TO SERVE:
few celery sticks, cut into small pieces
cauliflower florets
slices of French bread

American
2×2 oz cans anchovy filets
3–4 cloves garlic, chopped
4 tablespoons olive oil (approximately)
freshly ground black pepper
chopped fresh parsley to garnish
TO SERVE:
few celery stalks, cut into small pieces
cauliflower florets
slices of French bread

Drain the anchovies and place in a small pan with the garlic and oil. Leave to soften over a very low heat, stirring occasionally, for a few minutes. Remove from the heat and pound to a smooth paste, the consistency of thick cream; if too thick add a little more oil.

Turn into a bowl. Chill before serving, sprinkled with chopped parsley. Serve with the vegetables and French bread.
SERVES 6 TO 8

ASPERGES AUX DEUX SAUCES

Asparagus with Two Sauces

Metric/Imperial
1 kg/2 lb asparagus
salt
VINAIGRETTE:
1 small clove garlic, crushed
1 small shallot, finely chopped
1×5 ml spoon/1 teaspoon sugar
1×5 ml spoon/1 teaspoon French
    mustard
2–3×15 ml spoons/2–3 tablespoons
    chopped mixed fresh herbs
freshly ground white pepper
150 ml/¼ pint olive oil
1×15 ml spoon/1 tablespoon tarragon
    vinegar
1×15 ml spoon/1 tablespoon wine
    vinegar
2×15 ml spoons/2 tablespoons lemon
    juice

SAUCE MOUSSELINE:
300 ml/½ pint double cream
2 egg yolks
freshly ground black pepper
juice of 1 lemon

American
2 lb asparagus
salt
VINAIGRETTE:
1 small clove garlic, crushed
1 small shallot, finely chopped
1 teaspoon sugar
1 teaspoon French mustard
2–3 tablespoons chopped mixed fresh
    herbs
freshly ground white pepper
⅔ cup olive oil
1 tablespoon tarragon vinegar
1 tablespoon wine vinegar
2 tablespoons lemon juice
SAUCE MOUSSELINE:
1¼ cups heavy cream
2 egg yolks
freshly ground black pepper
juice of 1 lemon

Wash the asparagus carefully and cut off any woody parts from the stems. Lightly scrape the stems from tip to base. Cut the sticks to the same length and tie in bundles of 10 to 12. Stand these upright in a large pan of boiling salted water with the tips above the water. Cook until the tips are just tender; 12 to 15 minutes or longer, depending on thickness of stems. Drain.

For the *vinaigrette*; combine the garlic, shallot, sugar, mustard, herbs and seasoning. Beat in the oil gradually then stir in the vinegar and lemon juice.

For the sauce; place the cream and egg yolks in a bowl over hot water. Season with salt and pepper and whisk until thick and frothy. Whisk in the lemon juice.

Serve the asparagus cold, accompanied by the sauces, as an entrée.
SERVES 4

BROCHETTE DE MOULES

Mussels on Skewers

The generous use of olive oil, thyme and tomatoes gives this ubiquitous dish its Mediterranean flavour.

Metric/Imperial
1 onion, chopped
glass of white wine
1.5 kg/3–3½ lb mussels
225 g/8 oz salted belly pork
225 g/8 oz tomatoes, quartered
4 bay leaves
olive oil for basting
1×15 ml spoon/1 tablespoon chopped
    fresh thyme
salt and pepper

American
1 onion, chopped
glass of white wine
3–3½ lb mussels
½ lb salt pork
½ lb tomatoes, quartered
4 bay leaves
olive oil for basting
1 tablespoon chopped fresh thyme
salt and pepper

Place the onion and wine in a large pan and bring to the boil. Add the mussels and cook for 8 minutes or until they open; drain and remove shells.

Cut the pork into 2 cm/1 inch cubes. Thread the mussels, pork, tomatoes and bay leaves alternately onto 4 kebab skewers. Brush liberally with oil and sprinkle with thyme, salt and pepper. Cook under a preheated grill (broiler) for 5 minutes each side, basting frequently.
SERVES 4

PAN BAGNAT

Provençal Snack

This snack is well known to holidaymakers in Provence. If *petits pains* (rolls) are unobtainable, substitute suitable lengths of *ficelle* or *baguette* French loaves.

Metric/Imperial
4 petits pains
1 clove garlic, halved
olive oil for sprinkling
few tomatoes, sliced
1–2 red or green peppers, cored, seeded
    and sliced
1–2 onions, thinly sliced into rings
1 small can anchovy fillets, drained
handful of black olives, stoned and sliced
freshly ground black pepper

American
4 petits pains
1 clove garlic, halved
olive oil for sprinkling
few tomatoes, sliced
1–2 red or green peppers, cored, seeded
    and sliced
1–2 onions, thinly sliced into rings
1 small can anchovy filets, drained
handful of black olives, pitted and sliced
freshly ground black pepper

Cut the rolls in half lengthwise and rub cut surfaces with garlic. Sprinkle with olive oil. Pile remaining ingredients on flat half of each roll, sprinkling with pepper to taste. Top with the other half of bread and serve.
SERVES 4

Asperges aux Deux Sauces, Croustade de Pintadeau de Père Pantalay (page 90)

TARTE AMPHYTRITE

Seafood Flan

Use a selection of your favourite shellfish – scallops, prawns (shrimp), crayfish (écrevisse) tails for this flan.

Metric/Imperial
pâte demi-feuilletée (see recipe)
40 g/1½ oz butter
0.75 kg/1½ lb assorted shellfish, cooked and shelled
2 × 15 ml spoons/2 tablespoons Cognac
4 eggs
2 egg yolks
450 ml/¾ pint single cream
1 × 15 ml spoon/1 tablespoon tomato purée
1 clove garlic, crushed
1 × 15 ml spoon/1 tablespoon chopped fresh parsley
freshly ground black pepper
25 g/1 oz Gruyère or Cheddar cheese, grated
8 live Dublin Bay prawns (optional)

American
pâte demi-feuilletée (see recipe)
3 tablespoons butter
1½ lb assorted shellfish, cooked and shelled
2 tablespoons Cognac
4 eggs
2 egg yolks
2 cups light cream
1 tablespoon tomato paste
1 clove garlic, crushed
1 tablespoon chopped fresh parsley
freshly ground black pepper
¼ cup grated Gruyère or Cheddar cheese
8 live jumbo shrimp (optional)

Prepare the pâte demi-feuilletée according to the recipe given for Tarte aux Cailles (page 82). Roll out thinly and use to line a 30 cm/12 inch flan ring set on a baking sheet, or a 30 × 20 cm/12 × 8 inch shallow baking tin.

Heat the butter in a sauté pan and lightly sauté the shellfish, with the Cognac added, for 2 minutes. Cool slightly, then arrange in the pastry case.

Beat the eggs, egg yolks and cream together in a bowl. Blend in the tomato purée (paste), garlic and parsley. Season with pepper and pour over the fish. Sprinkle with grated cheese. If liked, garnish with Dublin Bay prawns (jumbo shrimp); previously cooked in boiling water for 10 to 15 minutes.

Bake the flan in a preheated moderately hot oven (200°C/400°F/Gas Mark 6) for 40 to 50 minutes or until golden brown and the filling has set. Serve hot, or cold with a crisp green salad.
SERVES 8

CROUSTADE DE PINTADEAU DE PÈRE PANTALAY

Guinea Fowl Pie

This pie can be made with any suitable bird; chicken, turkey or game.

Metric/Imperial
pâte demi-feuilletée (see recipe)
1 young guinea fowl, quartered
1 large onion, chopped
1 large carrot, chopped
4 × 15 ml spoons/4 tablespoons oil
2 × 15 ml spoons/2 tablespoons Cognac, warmed
150 ml/¼ pint dry white wine
200 ml/⅓ pint jellied chicken stock (see page 94)
1 × 15 ml spoon/1 tablespoon flour
salt
freshly ground black pepper
1 truffle, sliced and sautéed in butter (optional)
FORCEMEAT:
150 g/5 oz cooked chicken, minced
25 g/1 oz cooked ham, diced
25 g/1 oz mushrooms, chopped and sautéed in butter
3 × 15 ml spoons/3 tablespoons flour
3 × 15 ml spoons/3 tablespoons milk
4 × 5 ml spoons/4 teaspoons cream
1 egg yolk
beaten egg to glaze

American
pâte demi-feuilletée (see recipe)
1 young guinea fowl, quartered
1 large onion, chopped
1 large carrot, chopped
4 tablespoons oil
2 tablespoons Cognac, warmed
⅔ cup dry white wine
1 cup jellied chicken stock (see page 94)
1 tablespoon flour
salt
freshly ground black pepper
1 truffle, sliced and sautéed in butter (optional)
FORCEMEAT:
⅔ cup ground cooked chicken
2 tablespoons diced processed ham
¼ cup chopped mushrooms, sautéed in butter
3 tablespoons flour
3 tablespoons milk
4 teaspoons cream
1 egg yolk
beaten egg to glaze

Prepare the pâte demi-feuilletée according to the recipe given for Tarte aux Cailles (page 82); chill. Bone the guinea fowl. Place the bones in a roasting pan with the onion, carrot and oil and roast in a hot oven (230°C/450°F/Gas Mark 8) for 20 minutes or until well browned. Pour off 2 × 15 ml spoons/2 tablespoons fat into a saucepan and sauté the guinea fowl until golden brown; remove and set aside.

Pour Cognac over bone mixture and

Tarte Amphytrite

flambez. Add wine and jellied stock; cook over brisk heat for 10 minutes, then strain. Stir the flour into the fat remaining in the saucepan. Gradually blend in the strained sauce and cook, stirring, until smooth and thickened. Add salt and pepper to taste and truffle, if used. Remove from heat.

To make the forcemeat; mix the chicken, ham and mushrooms. Blend the flour with the milk, cream and egg yolk in a small pan. Stir over gentle heat until thick and creamy then mix in the meat mixture and seasoning to taste.

Roll out two-thirds of the pastry and use to line an 18–20 cm/7–8 inch deep pie dish or loose-bottomed cake tin. Press one half of the forcemeat into the pastry case. Place the pieces of guinea fowl on top and cover with remaining forcemeat.

Roll out remaining pastry to form a lid. Place over the pie, seal edges and trim. Brush with beaten egg and make a hole in the centre of the pie. Bake in a preheated hot oven (230°C/450°F/Gas Mark 8) for 20 to 30 minutes. Reheat the sauce and pour a little through the hole in the pastry; serve the remainder separately.
SERVES 4 TO 6

LAPIN PROVENÇAL

Provençal-Style Rabbit

Metric/Imperial
1 rabbit weighing about 1.5 kg/3–3½ lb
3 × 15 ml spoons/3 tablespoons oil
175 g/6 oz salted belly pork, diced
225 g/8 oz onions, sliced
1 red pepper, cored, seeded and sliced
1 green pepper, cored, seeded and sliced
0.5 kg/1 lb tomatoes, skinned, or
 1 × 425 g/15 oz can peeled tomatoes
2 × 15 ml spoons/2 tablespoons chopped
 mixed herbs (thyme, parsley, basil,
 marjoram)
2 × 5 ml spoons/2 teaspoons French
 mustard
salt
freshly ground black pepper

American
1 rabbit, weighing about 3–3½ lb
3 tablespoons oil
6 oz salt pork, diced
2 cups sliced onions
1 red pepper, cored, seeded and sliced
1 green pepper, cored, seeded and sliced
1 lb tomatoes, skinned, or 15 oz can
 peeled tomatoes
2 tablespoons chopped mixed herbs
 (thyme, parsley, basil, marjoram)
2 teaspoons French mustard
salt
freshly ground black pepper

Cut the rabbit into serving pieces; wash and dry thoroughly. Heat the oil in a sauté pan and fry pork briskly until evenly browned. Transfer pork to a large casserole. Add the rabbit to the sauté pan and brown on all sides. Place in the casserole.

Sauté the onions and peppers in the oil remaining in the pan until soft but not coloured. Add the tomatoes, herbs and mustard. Bring to the boil and pour over meats. Season to taste with salt and pepper.

Cover and cook in a preheated moderate oven (160°C/325°F/Gas Mark 3) for 1¼ hours or until rabbit is tender.
SERVES 4 TO 6

BLÉA TOURTE

Sweet Spinach Flan

Originally made with beet leaves, currants and pine kernels, *bléa tourte* has all but disappeared from restaurants in France.

Metric/Imperial
pâte brisée (see recipe)
FILLING:
350 g/12 oz spinach
salt
300 ml/½ pint milk
1 vanilla pod
50 g/2 oz sugar
25 g/1 oz plain flour
2 egg yolks
25 g/1 oz currants (optional)
2 × 15 ml spoons/2 tablespoons pine nut
 kernels (optional)
beaten egg to glaze
crystallized orange slices to decorate

Bléa Tourte

American
pâte brisée (see recipe)
FILLING:
¾ lb spinach
salt
1¼ cups milk
1 vanilla bean
¼ cup sugar
¼ cup all-purpose flour
2 egg yolks
3 tablespoons currants (optional)
2 tablespoons pine nut kernels
 (optional)
beaten egg to glaze
candied orange slices to decorate

Prepare the *pâte brisée* according to the recipe given for *Tarte à l'Oignon* (page 79), using half quantities. Rinse spinach, drain and place in a pan with a little salt. Cook covered, without additional liquid, for 5 to 10 minutes until tender. Cool.

Place the milk, vanilla and sugar in a saucepan and bring slowly to the boil, stirring. Remove from the heat and leave to infuse for 10 minutes before discarding the vanilla pod (bean). Blend flour with egg yolks and whisk in the warm milk. Return to the pan, bring to the boil, stirring constantly, and cook for 2 minutes. Allow to cool.

Roll out the pastry thinly and use to line a buttered 20 cm/8 inch flan ring set on a baking sheet. Stir the spinach into the custard, with the currants, if used. Spread over the pastry case and decorate with the pastry trimmings. Sprinkle with pine nut kernels, if used.

Brush with beaten egg and bake in a moderately hot oven (190°C/375°F/Gas Mark 5) for about 30 minutes. Decorate with crystallized (candied) orange slices and serve hot or warm.
SERVES 6

CRÊPES SOUFFLÉES À L'ORANGE

Fluffy Pancakes with Orange Sauce

Metric/Imperial
6 small crêpes (see page 18)
FILLING:
25 g/1 oz butter
25 g/1 oz flour
40 g/1½ oz sugar
7 × 15 ml spoons/7 tablespoons milk
2 eggs, separated
6 × 15 ml spoons/6 tablespoons Grand Marnier or Cointreau
SAUCE:
juice of 2 oranges and 1 lemon
finely grated rind of 1 orange
sugar to taste
TO SERVE:
4–5 × 15 ml spoons/4–5 tablespoons Grand Marnier or Cointreau, warmed

American
6 small crêpes (see page 18)
FILLING:
2 tablespoons butter
¼ cup flour
3 tablespoons sugar
7 tablespoons milk
2 eggs, separated
6 tablespoons Grand Marnier or Cointreau
SAUCE:
juice of 2 oranges and 1 lemon
finely grated rind of 1 orange
sugar to taste
TO SERVE:
4–5 tablespoons Grand Marnier or Cointreau, warmed

Prepare *crêpes* and set aside. For the filling; melt butter in a pan and stir in the flour and sugar. Blend in the milk and cook for 1 minute. Take off heat and beat in the egg yolks and liqueur. Whisk egg whites until stiff then fold into the mixture.

Spread evenly over the pancakes and fold each in half. Cook immediately in a preheated moderately hot oven (200°C/400°F/Gas Mark 6) for 6 to 8 minutes, until well risen.

Meanwhile mix all sauce ingredients together in a saucepan and simmer over moderate heat for about 3 minutes to reduce.

To serve; arrange pancakes on a hot serving dish and take immediately to the table. Pour on the warmed liqueur and *flambez*. Pour a little sauce over each pancake before serving.
SERVES 3

Oreillettes (left); Selection of Provençal olives in the street market of Hyéres (right)

OREILLETTES

Lenten Fritters

All over the southern strip of France, and especially during Lent, you will find these semi-sweet titbits. They come in all sorts of shapes and sizes. The plate-sized variety shown in our picture, looking rather like crystallized pancakes, came from the small town of St Gilles on the edge of the Camargue.

Metric/Imperial
15 g/½ oz yeast
3 × 15 ml spoons/3 tablespoons warm milk
450 g/1 lb plain flour
1 × 2.5 ml spoon/½ teaspoon salt
1 tablespoon sugar
4 eggs, beaten
grated rind of 1 lemon
few drops of vanilla essence
5 × 15 ml spoons/5 tablespoons rum or orange flower water
oil for shallow frying
icing sugar for dusting
strips of candied peel to decorate (optional)

American
½ cake compressed yeast
3 tablespoons warm milk
4 cups all-purpose flour
½ teaspoon salt
1 tablespoon sugar
4 eggs, beaten
grated rind of 1 lemon
few drops of vanilla extract
5 tablespoons rum or orange flower water
oil for shallow frying
confectioners' sugar for dusting
strips of candied peel to decorate (optional)

Chef Gabriel Rousselet serving the author with Crêpes Soufflées a l'Orange

Cream the yeast with the warm milk. Sift the flour and salt into a large bowl. Stir in the sugar. Make a well in the centre and add the yeast liquid, eggs, lemon rind, vanilla and rum. Beat to a smooth, soft dough. Leave, covered, in a warm place for about 2 hours or until well risen.

Knead briefly, then break off egg-sized pieces and roll lightly into rounds, about half the diameter of your frying pan (skillet). Leave in a warm place for 10 to 15 minutes.

Heat a little oil in the pan. Take each round in turn and, using the fingertips, stretch it thinly to fit the pan. Fry over brisk heat until crisp and puffy, turning once. Drain on kitchen paper. Sprinkle with sugar. Decorate with candied peel.
MAKES ABOUT 18

Glossary

BAKE BLIND, TO
To bake a pastry case before filling. The pastry case is lined with foil or greaseproof (waxed) paper, weighted down with dried beans, and cooked in a moderately hot oven (200°C/400°F/Gas Mark 6) for about 15 minutes.

BEURRE MANIÉ
Equal quantities of butter and flour kneaded together with a fork and used for thickening sauces, soups and casseroles.

BOUQUET GARNI
A selection of herbs (parsley, thyme, bay etc.) tied together or enclosed in a muslin (cheesecloth) bag. Used for flavouring soups, casseroles and sauces.

DÉGLACEZ
To dilute pan juices with wine, cider or cream to make gravy; the pan is constantly stirred and scraped to mix the juices.

FLAMBEZ
To pour warmed alcohol (brandy, liqueur etc.) over food while cooking, set alight and stir until flames have died down.

FLEURON
Small puff pastry crescent, used to garnish dishes.

JULIENNE
Vegetable cut into small 'matchstick' strips; frequently used as a garnish.

MARINATE, TO
To steep raw meat, fish, poultry or game in a liquor such as wine, alcohol, oil or vinegar; usually flavoured with herbs and spices. Used to tenderize and flavour the food.

MIREPOIX
A mixture of finely diced vegetables to which chopped ham may be added. It is cooked gently in butter.

REDUCE, TO
To concentrate a liquid by boiling and evaporation. The reduction in volume may also be achieved by prolonged simmering.

ROUX
A mixture of butter and flour, cooked and used as a base for sauces.

SEASONING
Salt and pepper are added to food to enhance flavour. Most French chefs use *gros sel* or *sel gris* rather than table salt; sea salt, which is readily available, is ideal. Pepper should always be freshly ground. Black pepper is suitable for most purposes. For delicately flavoured sauces and dishes use white pepper. Green pepper adds a fresh taste but is not widely available.

STOCKS AND SAUCES
Good quality *fonds* or stocks are important, if not essential, in French cooking. Home-made stocks provide body as well as flavour. Stocks prepared from (bouillon) cubes will add flavour to dishes but not the required texture.
Home-made stocks freeze well. They will also keep for up to 4 days in the refrigerator but should be re-boiled every 2 days.

FOND DE VOLAILLE (CHICKEN STOCK) Place a raw chicken carcass in a large pan together with the giblets, any scraps of meat, 1 sliced onion, 2 sliced carrots, 1 chopped leek, bouquet garni, few white peppercorns, salt and 2.75 litres/5 pints (U.S. 6 pints) water. Bring to the boil, cover and simmer very gently for 2 to 3 hours. Strain and, when cold, skim off the fat. MAKES ABOUT 2 LITRES/3½ PINTS (U.S. 4½ PINTS).

FOND BLANC (VEAL STOCK) Blanch a 1 kg/2¼ lb veal knuckle (shank end) in boiling water for 10 minutes. Drain and place in a large pan with 2 sliced onions, 2 sliced carrots, 1–2 sticks celery, chopped; bouquet garni, few white peppercorns, salt and a squeeze of lemon juice. Pour in 2.75 litres/5 pints (U.S. 6 pints) water. Bring to the boil, cover and simmer gently for 2 to 3 hours. Strain, cool and skim off fat. MAKES ABOUT 2 LITRES/3½ PINTS (U.S. 4½ PINTS).

JELLIED VEAL OR CHICKEN STOCK Prepare stock as above then simmer, partially covered, until reduced by about half. MAKES ABOUT 1 LITRE/1¾ PINTS (U.S. 2¼ PINTS).

FOND BRUN (BROWN STOCK) Proceed as for *fond blanc*, but after blanching the veal bones, drain and place in a roasting pan. Cook in a preheated hot oven (220°C/425°F/ Gas Mark 7) for about 40 minutes, turning occasionally, until evenly browned. Place the browned bones in a large pan, add remaining ingredients and continue as for *fond blanc*. MAKES ABOUT 2 LITRES/3½ PINTS (U.S. 4½ PINTS).

GLACE DE VIANDE (MEAT JELLY) Prepare a *fond brun* and continue to simmer, uncovered, skimming frequently and stirring occasionally. The *glace de viande* is ready when the stock has reduced to a thick syrupy consistency and is a rich brown colour. It is used as a meat glaze and to add flavour and gloss to certain sauces.

DEMI-GLACE Prepare Espagnole sauce according to the recipe given for *Caneton à la Bigarade* (page 46). Stir in 2–3 × 15 ml spoons/2–3 tablespoons *glace de viande*. For recipes requiring small quantities, substitute *fond brun* if you do not have any *demi-glace* ready made.

COURT-BOUILLON Place 1 kg/2 lb rinsed fish trimmings (head, skin, bones etc.) in a large pan with 750 ml/1¼ pints/ 3 cups water. Add 200 ml/⅓ pint/1 cup dry white wine. Add 2 sliced carrots, 1 sliced onion, 1 crushed clove garlic, sprig of thyme, 2–3 bay leaves, few parsley sprigs and salt and black pepper to taste. Bring to the boil, cover and simmer for 20 minutes. Strain through a fine sieve or cloth. MAKES ABOUT 900 ML/1½ PINTS/3¾ CUPS.

FISH STOCK Place 0.75 kg/1½ lb rinsed fish trimmings (head, skin, bones etc.) in a large pan with 750 ml/1¼ pints/3 cups lightly salted water. Add 1 sliced onion and a bouquet garni. Bring slowly to the boil, cover and simmer gently for 30 minutes. Strain through a fine sieve or cloth. MAKES ABOUT 750 ML/1¼ PINTS/3 CUPS.

CLARIFYING STOCK Pour the stock into a large pan and add 1 lightly beaten egg white to each 1 litre/1¾ pints/4¼ cups stock. Heat gently, whisking constantly, until a thick froth forms. Lower heat, cover and simmer gently for 1½ hours. Strain through a double layer of muslin (cheesecloth).

BÉCHAMEL SAUCE Place 300 ml/½ pint/1¼ cups milk in a saucepan with ½ bay leaf, sprig of thyme, 1 small onion and a generous pinch of grated nutmeg. Bring slowly to the boil, take off the heat, cover and leave to infuse for 15 minutes. Melt 25 g/1 oz/2 tablespoons butter in another saucepan. Stir in 25 g/1 oz/¼ cup flour and cook for 2 minutes. Strain the milk and gradually add to the roux, stirring. Bring to the boil, stirring, and cook for 2 to 3 minutes. Adjust seasoning and stir in 2–3 × 15 ml spoons/2–3 tablespoons cream, if a rich sauce is required. MAKES 300 ML/½ PINT/1¼ CUPS.

Acknowledgments

We should like to extend our thanks to everyone who has helped us on our trips to France during the preparation of this book – hoteliers, restaurateurs, chefs, regional tourist board officials, members of *Syndicats d'initiatives* and a wide range of individuals.

Our special gratitude is due to the following:

Emil Arcé, *Hotel du Trinquet*, St-Etienne-de-Baïgorry*
Noël Arin, *Auberge de Kérank, Plouharnel*
François Bernard, *Jacques Coeur*, Bourges*
Michel Bernard, *Hotel du Dauphin*, L'Aigle*
Jacques Billet, *Moulin de Ferrières, Ferrières*
Georges Blanc, *Chez la Mère Blanc**, Vonnas*
Mlle Bonnet, *Hotel Bonnet, Beynac*
Adolphe Bosser, *Hotel le Goyen, Audierne*
Gérard Bruère, *Hotel Styvel, Camaret-sur-Mer*
Bernard Champion, *Auberge Chantecler*, Bourth*
Louis Chanuet, *Hotel Moderne*, Cluny*
Château de Castel Novel**, Varetz, Nr Brive
Hotel Cro-Magnon*, Les Eyzies
Claude Darroze, *Chez Darroze*, Langon*
Jean Dartix, *Au Grand St-Martin, Ivry-la-Bataille*
Michel Dauven, *Auberge du Soir, Brantôme*
Hotel Davat, Aix-les-Bains
Domaine de l'Abbaye, Bernardvillé
Paul Fagoaga, *Hotel Arraya*, Sare*
Jean-Michel Flavel, *Restaurant au Marais, Coulon*
René Floranc, *Au Père Floranc*, Wettolsheim*
Michel Garrigou, *Hotel St-Albert, Sarlat*
M. Geyer, *Aux Trois Roses, la Petite Pierre*
Grand Hotel de Roquefort, Roquefort-sur-Soulzon
La Grange aux Moines, Plage de Kerouanno
Maurice Isabel, *Hotel Ithurria*, Ainhoa*
André Jeunet, *Hotel de Paris*, Arbois*
L. Le Moigne (Maître Pâtissier), *Douarnenez*
Auberge Maître Corbeau*, Ezy-sur-Eure
Jean-Paul Male, *Auberge St-Jean*, St-Jean-de-Blaignac*
Hotel Marine, Tancarville
Alain Masbou (Pâtissier), *Capdenac*
Pierre Maurel, *Brûleur de Loups, Stes-Maries-de-la-Mer*
Pierre Maurenc (Pâtissier), *St-Gilles*
Mme Huguette Mazet, *le Cellier de Bonaguil, Château de Bonaguil*
Marc Meneau, *l'Espérance**, St-Pere-de-Vezelay*
Jean-Pierre Michel, *la Regalido*, Fontvieille*
Jean-Marie Miquel, *Hotel Miquel, Najac*
Mme Marie-Thérèse Neuville, *Auberge le Pré-Bossu, Moudeyres*
Mlles Peyrac, *Cantou Fleuri, Salers*
Louis-Francis Pommier, *le Petit Coq au Champs*, Campigny*
Gabriel Rousselet, *Les Bories*, Gordes*
Julian Savy, *Hotel Moderne, Rodez*
Jean-Claude Scaviner, *Manoir d'Hastings*, Bénouville*
Mme Sergent, *Auberge de l'Abbaye*, le Bec-Hellouin*
La Terrasse au Soleil, Ceret
G. Thibault, *Ostellerie de Vieux Péroges*, Pérouges*
Walter Tinelli, *Le Pothuau, Port Pothuau, Nr Hyères*
Jean-Pierre Vullin, *Auberge Bressane**, Bourg-en-Bresse*
Denis Weller, *Hotel des Vosges, Obernai*

(* designates quality of food and service; as awarded in Michelin Guide)

Index